Note-Taking
Made Easy

DATE DUE

Other Books by Judi Kesselman-Turkel and Franklynn Peterson:

BOOKS IN THIS SERIES

The Grammar Crammer: How to Write Perfect Sentences
Research Shortcuts
Secrets to Writing Great Papers
Spelling Simplified
Study Smarts: How to Learn More in Less Time
Test-Taking Strategies
*The Vocabulary Builder: The Practically Painless Way to a
    Larger Vocabulary*

OTHER COAUTHORED BOOKS FOR ADULTS

The Author's Handbook
The Do-It-Yourself Custom Van Book (with Dr. Frank Konishi)
Eat Anything Exercise Diet (with Dr. Frank Konishi)
Good Writing
Homeowner's Book of Lists
The Magazine Writer's Handbook

COAUTHORED BOOKS FOR CHILDREN

I Can Use Tools
Vans

BY JUDI KESSELMAN-TURKEL

Stopping Out: A Guide to Leaving College and Getting Back In

BY FRANKLYNN PETERSON

The Build-It-Yourself Furniture Catalog
Children's Toys You Can Build Yourself
Freedom from Fibromyalgia (with Nancy Selfridge, M.D.)
Handbook of Lawn Mower Repair
Handbook of Snowmobile Maintenance and Repair
How to Fix Damn Near Everything
How to Improve Damn Near Everything around Your Home

Note-Taking Made Easy

Judi Kesselman-Turkel
and
Franklynn Peterson

The University of Wisconsin Press

The University of Wisconsin Press
1930 Monroe Street
Madison, Wisconsin 53711

www.wisc.edu/wisconsinpress/

3 Henrietta Street
London WC2E 8LU, England

5   4   3   2   1

Printed in the United States of America

Library of Congress Cataloging-in-Publication Data
Kesselman-Turkel, Judi.
    Note-taking made easy / Judi Kesselman-Turkel and Franklynn Peterson.
    p. cm.
    Originally published: Chicago : Contemporary Books, ©1982.
    ISBN 0-299-19154-0 (pbk. : alk. paper)
    1. Note-taking—Handbooks, manuals, etc. I. Peterson, Franklynn. II. Title.
LB2395.25.K47   2003
378'.170281—dc21   2003050113

Contents

1. There's No Substitute for Taking Your Own Good
   Notes   *1*
   Note-Taking Helps You Pay Attention
   Note-Taking Helps You Remember
   Good Note-Taking Helps Organize Ideas
2. How to Tell What's Worth Noting   *7*
   Criteria for Deciding What's Worth Preserving
      1. Category: What Type of Information Is It?
      2. Relevance: Does the Information Relate to the
         Topic?
      3. Importance: Do You Need the Information?
      4. Personal Bias: Do You Want to Remember the
         Information?
   Aids That Put Your Notes in Perspective
      1. Buy, Borrow, or Make a Course Outline
      2. Start Learning the Course Jargon

3. How to Organize Notes   *24*
    How to Use Outline Form
    How to Work Outline Form into a Memory Clue
        System
    How to Use Patterning to Organize Notes
4. Shortcuts for Note-Taking   *37*
    Use of Shorthand for Quicker Note-Taking
5. Taking Notes from Assigned Text   *41*
    Learn How to Read for a Course
        1. How to Skim
    How to Take Notes from Fiction
    How to Take Textbook Notes
        1. Size Up the Textbook
        2. Systematize Your Note-Taking with OK4R
    How to Take Notes on Nontextbook Nonfiction
    Learn How to Write in Your Books
        1. Use the Margin—Sparingly
        2. Note Significant Pages in the Front Inside Cover
        3. Put Important Data at the End of the Book
    A Word about Other Note-Taking Systems
6. Taking Lecture Notes   *54*
    Listening vs. Reading
    Organize Your Tools
    Keep Your Course Outline Handy
    Keep Your Mind from Wandering
        1. Choose a Seat Carefully
        2. Avoid Friends
        3. Keep Lecture and Personal Matters Separate
        4. Stay Awake, Stay Alert
    Catch the Lecturer's Clues
        1. Relate the Lecture to Your Assigned Reading
        2. Keep Track of Time
        3. Listen for Speaking Style
        4. Keep Alert for the Lecturer's Special Words
7. Taking Research Notes   *64*
    Preparing a Preliminary Outline
    Listing Research Questions

Using Good Note-Taking Tools
1. Prepare a Work File
2. Prepare Bibliography Blanks
3. Key Your Notes to the Bibliography Blanks
4. Note Which Page Numbers Your Notes Came From
5. Key Each Photocopy
Keeping Notes Legible
Taking Adequate Notes
8. Taking Minutes of Meetings   *75*

Appendix A: Notes on Chapter 1   *79*
Appendix B: Practice in Analyzing Information and Taking Notes on Lectures   *81*
Appendix C: Course Outline for "Methods of Note-Taking"   *91*
Appendices D and E: Speech Outline and Speech Clue Words   *93*
Appendix F: Shorthand Notes on Chapter 4   *95*
Appendix G: "Agent X" Research Questions   *97*

The one ingredient most basic to school success is the ability to take good notes. To concentrate on developing that ability, this book combines, expands, and adds greatly to a number of pointers that have been discussed, in other contexts, in this series' companion books *Study Smarts* and *Research Shortcuts,* so that students may have, in one convenient volume, all the help they need.

1

There's No Substitute for Taking Your Own Good Notes

Walk around any college campus, or take a fast stab at surfing the Internet, and soon you'll find a place to buy notes for nearly any course. The buying and selling of course notes has become big business, and mostly they're thorough, well-organized notes taken by A students.

Do they guarantee the buyer an A? Not on your life. In fact, if the buyer attempts to use them instead of taking her own notes, *we* guarantee that she'll probably get no more than a C.

Sit inside any lecture hall for a few minutes, and soon you'll notice the tape recorder addicts. While you and many others are scribbling a mile a minute, these students seem to have it taped. They sit back and let their recorders catch every word.

Does taping take the place of note taking? Not a chance.

It practically guarantees twice the work for lower grades.

The painful truth is, there's no substitute for taking your own good notes. Before we look at the reasons, find pen and paper so you can take notes on the rest of the chapter. (To evaluate your note-taking ability, compare your notes with ours in Appendix A.)

NOTE-TAKING HELPS YOU PAY ATTENTION

We've all got more things on our minds than the text we're reading or the lecture we're listening to. There's last night's good or bad time, tomorrow's exam, the paper that's due, or the phone call that needs to be made. If we don't actively keep extraneous thoughts out, they'll creep in and distract us from noticing significant facts and ideas. Most students we've seen in lectures with turned-on tape recorders look glassy-eyed and far away. Many students with prepackaged note packets let their minds wander when they're reading, figuring the notes will cover for them. But a tape recorder may garble an important phrase if someone coughs nearby, and its batteries always fail at the least welcome time. And someone else's notes are based on someone else's previous knowledge. If she's known for ages how to work with negative numbers, her notes on that lesson will be sketchy and inferential, and if you count on them pulling you through the first exam, you may be up the creek.

We can't understand _why_ students tape lectures. Even in our professional interviewing, we rarely rely on recorders. They're not only unreliable, they're a waste of time. To find out what's important, a student has to listen to the tape again without the lecturer's body language to help him decipher the words. If he doesn't take notes on _this_ rehearing, he spends more wasted hours playing the tape over and over—and trying to unravel unfamiliar and slurred words. If you've taken to taping lectures, the quickest grade-raiser would be to bury your tape recorder deep in a dresser drawer.

NOTE-TAKING HELPS YOU REMEMBER

Students spend countless hours trying to get facts into their heads, thinking that that's where all the remembering occurs. But our *muscles* really have better memories than our heads. We once watched a 68-year-old man climb on a bike for the first time in 40 years and, after a few tentative starts, ride off down to the corner. Though his brain was able to recall less than 10 percent of all the facts he'd learned during his first 28 years, his muscles had about 90 percent recall.

Note-taking is a muscle activity. The very act of note-taking helps you remember the ideas you're writing down. It's much more efficient than just listening or reading, even if you're the most attentive person in the world.

Some students are convinced that they can't concentrate on what they're reading or hearing when they're taking notes. Often, it's because their note-taking skills are poor. They race to take down every word, unable to sort out what belongs in their notes. They have developed few shortcuts.

Some students think they miss the continuity of what's being read or said when they're taking notes. But experiments show that you miss a lot more if you listen to a whole lecture or read an entire chapter and then try to remember its important points.

GOOD NOTE-TAKING HELPS ORGANIZE IDEAS

Students' notes we've seen fall into three general categories: overzealous, undeveloped, and just right. Here are examples of the three types. Which type do your notes look most like?

Overzealous

LECTURE 1: MONEY AND INTEREST   9/2/82

1. Period, principal, interest, amount
   The amount charged to a borrower by a lender for the use of money over a *period* of time is called *interest*. The sum loaned is called the *principal*. The sum of the principal and the interest is called the *amount*. The amount is usually payable at the end of the *period*.

2. To determine interest
   The amount of interest is usually determined as a function of the principal, length of time period, and a quantity called the interest rate. There are two kinds of interest, simple and compound.

3. Simple interest
   Simple interest is interest proportional to the original principal (P) and length of time period (t). $I = Prt$ when r is the rate of simple interest per unit of time. If t is measured in years, r is the annual rate of simple interest.
   Example: What amount must be invested at 7.5% per year simple interest to yield $250 interest after 3 months?

$$I = Prt, \text{ so } P = I/rt$$
$$P = \$250/(.075)(\tfrac{1}{4}) = \$13333\tfrac{1}{3}$$

4. Compound interest
                    [*etc.*]

Undeveloped

Int = chg for using money over time per
Prin = sum loaned
Amt usually payable end of per
Take cat to vet for shots
Int = Prin × lngth of time × int rate
Simple int = ditto
John, lend me your calculator
P = $250/.075 × ¼ =

Compound Int =
add int to amt, = prin in nxt t
[*etc.*]

Just Right

Main Topic: Kinds of Interest

1. Definitions
   I = Interest = amt charged for borrowing money
   P = Principal = sum loaned
   t = time period = time of loan
   r = rate of simple int per unit of time
       (i.e. if t = years, r = annual rate)
   Amount (usually payable at end of period) = prin + int
   n = number of time periods in term of transaction

2. Simple interest
   Formula: I = Prt

ex. ? invested at 7.5% per yr simple int yields $250 in 3 mos?

$$P = I/rt$$
$$P = \$250/(.075)(\frac{1}{4})$$

3. Compound interest
   Formula: $S_n = P (1 \times r)^n$

   [*etc.*]

The first example is excerpted from a 90-page booklet of photocopied lecture notes that was being sold—and not cheaply—at our local university's photocopy center. We wouldn't buy it unless: (a) there was no assigned textbook and (b) we planned to skip all the lectures. Wading through it would be almost like—though not as accurate as—reading the textbook. Some students feel compelled, as this one was, to copy down every word in the order it was said or read. Organization is totally lacking. Just because notes are for sale doesn't mean they're good notes. In fact, they're *usually* overwritten so that even the slowest student can understand them, and they're often underorganized.

Example 2 is taken from a page of a D student's notes for the same lecture. You can see where his mind was much of the time.

Example 3 is an A student's notes. It's easy to see why. Good note-taking is not only thorough, it's *organized*. And, as we hope we've convinced you, there's no substitute for taking your own good notes. If you've taken notes on this chapter, as we suggested at the beginning, which example do they most resemble? Compare them now with our version in Appendix A to further pinpoint your note-taking weaknesses.

2

How to Tell What's Worth Noting

If you're like most students, you've probably been taking notes for three-quarters of your life without stopping to figure out what you're doing and why. And your notes probably look it, too: a jumble of facts, figures, sentences, and paragraphs in no particular order using no particular system. If challenged, you can probably come up with several general explanations for why you take notes: so you can do well on the next exam, so you can get a good grade, so you can remember what you heard or read. But if asked why you copied one word instead of another, one thought instead of several equally interesting (or boring) ones, would you know what to answer?

If you're one of the lucky few who did, sometime in your early grades, get some formal training in how to take notes, you've probably forgotten most of what you learned. What to look and listen for, why to jot down one particular phrase instead of another, how to write quickly and still keep your notes easy to read: these are the skills that make for high grades.

Before we tackle the mechanics of *how* to put notes on paper, let's look at *what* to copy down. The word *notable,* which is usually used to mean "distinguished," began its life meaning "worthy of note"—in other words, worth preserving by taking notes on its existence. So there's one main question that should be asked of any idea we read or hear: is it notable? In other words, is it worth preserving?

CRITERIA FOR DECIDING WHAT'S WORTH PRESERVING

There are four criteria for deciding whether or not something is noteworthy: its *c*ategory, *r*elevance, and *im*portance; and your personal *b*ias. (To remember them, think CRIB as in *crib notes.*) As you read or listen, you should be considering all four criteria. Put the following questions to yourself.

1. Category: What Type of Information Is It?

All information can be divided into two main categories: facts and opinions. Make sure you can tell the difference.

A. Facts

A fact is a true statement. Some facts are *self-evident,* like the fact that snow is wet. Some facts are factual by *definition,* like the fact that there are 12 inches in a foot. But most of the facts you'll be taking notes on are *proven* facts: facts that have been established by *evidence.*

For defined and self-evident facts, your notes need contain only the facts. But for proven facts, you must, in most cases, also jot down the evidence. Some kinds of evidence are:

- *Authority:* If a well-respected individual who ought to know says that a fact is so, that's often adequate proof. If the source of a fact is an authoritative journal or book, that's proof enough. The catchword here is *authoritative.* Though the *Reader's Digest* may be authoritative enough for a third-grader, it's completely unacceptable for a college student.
- *Scientific research:* If carefully conducted scientific research shows that the information is factual, that's proof enough. Cite the research in your notes.
- *Corroboration:* If several reliable sources reported something as fact, that's often—but not always—proof enough if you can cite the sources. But be careful: just because two people *believe* the same thing doesn't automatically make the belief factual. Look at how many people once believed the Earth was flat.

B. Opinions

Anything people believe without proof is not fact, it's opinion. If it's an opinion held within a person's scope of authority, it is an *informed* opinion, but it's opinion nonetheless. If Buckminster Fuller were to say, "It's possible that some day we'll all live in dome homes," that would be opinion even though it came from the originator of geodesic domes.

Read or listen closely, and look for clues that signal opinions: *qualifiers* like *maybe, possibly, in all likelihood,* and other carefully selected words. In the following passage, we've italicized the words that should signal that nothing in the paragraph is hard fact.

> You *may* have *heard* that viruses cause cancer. *Suggested* by researchers as a *question*—not an answer—some years ago, this *theory* quickly was *espoused* by physicians, patients, and especially the

popular press. It was a pleasant *theory* to *believe; if* a virus caused cancer, an inoculation that *would* prevent or cure it *had to be* just around the corner.

For some courses, opinions don't count. Though a lecturer may offer many other people's opinions and some of his own, none of them need go into your notes. For other courses, opinion may be very important. Either you'll have to rely on your own good sense to decide whether opinions must be noted, or ask the instructor for guidelines.

Exercise

Even when delivering a prepared text, a good lecturer relaxes the language, inserts details and asides, and eliminates boring citations in order to keep his listeners interested. The following speech excerpt* is an excellent example of this. Underline the words that signal opinion. For every fact, cite the kinds of evidence presented by the author. (Appendix B has the answers to this exercise.)

We historians are not in vogue nowadays, so when I have an audience even semi-captured like this it's an inviting, enticing kind of situation to be in. But this *is* going to be a history lecture and I hope some of you will be transported nostalgically to your past history.

In an obvious state of rancor, Gloria Steinem, appearing recently before the National Press Club, called President Nixon the most sexually insecure chief of state since Napoleon. Ms. Steinem's remark was her reaction to the President's less than enthusiastic stand, we are told, on women's liberation. This contretemps points up a subject, I think, little studied by the social

*Excerpted from the speech "Eros in the White House" by Dr. Milton Plesur, Professor of History, State University of New York at Buffalo.

historian who after all is concerned primarily with mores, morals, and in general what we call popular culture. Despite the disdain Americans claim they have for history and the assertions of popular intellectuals and others that the discipline is irrelevant to today's action, I think most Americans are down deep and maybe even in a sublimated way lovers of the past. Legends or facts about our chief executives, true stories or fascinating gossip, and unfortunately even salacious banter, excite both the curious and the scholarly. Gore Vidal has stated in a recent review, I believe it was of the excellent book about Franklin and Eleanor Roosevelt by Joseph Lash, he stated in a recent *New York Review of Books* article that there exists a large public curiosity as to the happenings in the White House bedrooms or even in the corridors outside. The world is fascinated by the exploits of the famous and since sexuality obviously colors our lives, since it affords a unique insight into a person, president or not, I think it's the duty of the student to also explore this aspect of presidential lifestyle.

One of the trends of my discipline, not that I really understand it that much, is the study of psychohistory. And ever since Sigmund Freud, of course, sex has been the major part of the psychic profile that now, years later, historians are developing concerns with.

If a politician behaves in a certain way in his private life, there's a possibility that he could act in a similar vein publicly. And, of course, private indiscretions can eventually affect public policy. The famous example of Charles Stuart Parnell in Ireland being named a corespondent in a divorce suit probably hurt his whole program of home loan, but thus far his latterday colleague Bernadette Devlin doesn't seem to have her public life blighted by her private life. If we're looking for examples, there are many in history.

Today's society has been called the most permissive one in modern history, and while there is still a greater expectation of higher morality, I think, in the national leader, and the tendency to equate public greatness with private goodness, there is also more tolerance of a politician's personal weakness. Certainly people tend to overlook what they want to overlook. Some politicians, in other words, have fared better than others. Perhaps the presidential libido can even be rationalized, since men at the top are reputed to have very strong drives of many kinds or else they would not have achieved that eminence. And then there's also the unprecedented strain on the man in public life, in essence, which could explain, perhaps, the need for private release. I didn't explore that in a previous article on presidential health, and if I put these two papers together, the one on physical health and this on sexual health, I may go into this more.

But despite all that I have said was so important about sexuality in further understanding the President, the richness of psychoanalytic speculation is not matched by the historical evidence. We live in an age of media, and the less responsible of members of the press have always scrutinized, sometimes in very indelicate ways, every aspect of the presidential image.

You know, the president is no more than an elected king as far as many Americans are concerned and we are obviously fascinated by every little detail and every little fact, and perhaps the more salacious ones are more important to the layman than perhaps items of policy. The man in public life has not been entitled to an exclusive private life, and whispering galleries work overtime in producing rumors of politicians' possible real and imagined sexual derelictions. The American president is usually pretty well insulated against excessively prying eyes. There were at least two presidents for whom we now have fairly good documentation about their extramarital sexual affairs. Warren G. Harding used the Secret Service evidently to watch over his White House frolics, and while the second Roosevelt's marriage was almost broken up over his dalliance, it was kept out of print. The stories about John Kennedy's fascination with pretty girls were common Washington stories, but no scandal ever ensued. And I would predict, even though historians ought not to, that it would probably take a long time for any scandal to break.

Cleveland's victory was due in part to the blemished reputation of his adversary and to his own spotless record. As President, at the age of 49, his marriage to a 22-year-old girl in the year 1886 aroused great comment. In fact, I think, a lot of the society columnists were a little aggravated and tiffed because they thought that he was going to marry the girl's mother. Instead he married her. Mean gossips were full of gossip about beauty and the beast, but the marriage was a fine one and there was nothing to indicate anything but an exemplary moral life. Indeed, he sired his last child at the age of 70. He died the next year.

Woodrow Wilson complained of his ignorance of women and yet he was reputed to be a man of strong passion. His only real sexual interest was the woman he married in 1885. There were persisting stories about Mr. Wilson, especially in the few months after his wife died, but no story was more exciting than his romance with a 43-year-old beautiful widow, Edith Bolling Gault. Wilson proposed marriage to her. During this ardent courtship, he was criticized for emphasizing affairs of the heart and neglecting those of state. Some of his daily letters to Mrs. Gault were 20 pages in length. Now that took time, I suppose, away from the presidential burden.

Now this next section is going to deal with those presidents about whom there are interesting stories, about whom there may be implications and suspicions—although I add that the supportive evidence is weak and much of what I'm going to say is pre-presidential in chronology.

George Washington first, naturally. He was described by most of his biographers as an awkward and an unsuccessful young lover, a condition that for the most part, as I read about Washington, did not improve with his age. A critical biographer, writing incidentally in the debunking era of the 1920s, actually theorized that Washington's idealization of women was in fact a disappointment to most women because, according to this amateur and maybe frustrated psychologist, women do not like this kind of behavior. Washington's many letters are replete with references to frustrating experiences and therefore he felt wise enough to give advice on love and sex and marriage, and if time permitted I could read to you from some of those letters. Possibly his major sexual interest was the wife of a dear friend, Mrs. Sally Fairfax. Forty years after their initial meeting (George didn't give up too easily), he wrote her in Paris.

I think it is interesting to point out that Washington, Jefferson, and Madison all married widows. Maybe I'll have more to say about that later.

A lengthy article talks about Washington's subliminal relationships with his own brother, an older brother that died when Washington was just 20, with a frontiersman with whom he served, and even with Alexander Hamilton, but I don't think we should push these points by any means. These were certainly hardly consummated relationships.

John Adams, with typical honesty, admitted that he thoroughly enjoyed the fair sex. Although Adams appears to have been quite a ladies' man—he used to recite ovids to the art of love to various people—he claimed, "No virgin or matron ever had cause to blush at the sight of me or to regret her acquaintance with me. No father, brother, son, or friend ever had cause for grief or resentment for any intercourse between me and any daughter, sister, mother, or any other relation of the female sex." Now there isn't any other president who has written anything that definitive, though I'm sure there are many that could have.

Thomas Jefferson—his love affairs have been well documented. Though they were generally unsuccessful, there was at least one that seemed serious—this is the famous Walker affair—so much so that a generation afterwards he acknowledged his guilt and the incorrectness of offering "love to a handsome lady." In 1772 he married a widow. While it was a happy marriage, Mrs. Jefferson was sick for the ten years that they were married. There were, however, persistent rumors and reports of his use of female slaves. One such instance that gained tremendous notoriety was the affair with a slave girl named Sally Hennings. His political opposition, of course, made much of this affair. Now Sally Hennings bore him, so we think, between three and five children. In Jefferson's will there is the well-known provision that there will be five slaves emancipated—I assume Sally and four of her offspring.

Abraham Lincoln is one of the most thoroughly researched presidents. According to William Herndon, his ex-law partner, and not the best source, Lincoln had a terribly strong passion for women and even a powerful lust. The oft-told story of his visit to a lady of the night reflects also his basic sense of values and honesty. I hope none of this alarms any of you people who think that I'm doing disservice to President Lincoln. It seems as if he didn't have enough money for the transaction, and when she offered to trust him for the difference, he said that he could not go on credit and he left with his mission incomplete. I don't know if this is the beginning of the phrase "Honest Abe" or not, but it certainly could have been.

Now, this is a story that has been told with some degree of plausibility in a respectable historian's work on Lincoln called *The Lincoln Nobody Knows,* by Professor Richard Kirk.

Now the last president that I want to say something about is the murdered John Kennedy, this despite the fact that in Camelot, as you know, the weather must be perfect all the year. Now we know that it is not completely perfect because anybody with the name of Kennedy is fair copy. Senator Ted Kennedy's Chappaquiddick adventure jolted many Americans, but one article stated that half of the women didn't believe what had happened at Chappaquiddick and the other half were dying to forgive him. Jackie's halo has become somewhat tarnished since the marriage to Onassis, the photos of her sporting a no-bra look, and her jet-set lifestyle. Because the President's life ended tragically, and since he has grown larger in death, Americans prefer to disregard the threatening clouds hovering over his area of Camelot. His younger days were spent in the shadow of an older brother, Joe. He and fellow Senator George Smathers of Florida were reputed to have far outdistanced all competitors in romantic conquests. Certainly the society columns linked this most eligible bachelor with very attractive society belles. And then there's the revelation of his long-time secretary Evelyn Lincoln, who said that one of her duties was to arrange for dates.

The bachelor's life, of course, ended with that dream marriage to Jacqueline Bouvier, but it is doubtful that the good life ended for either of them. The frequent absences of each from the other seemed to fuel notions of those that saw in the marriage a less than perfect liaison. A contemporary journalist only recently revived the old story about John Kennedy's supposed relationship with Marilyn Monroe. The movie star was even supposed to have credited her peculiar talents for making his back feel better—that's a direct quote. I'd sure like to be the historian that finds the sources on this one.

But the implications of the Kennedy story illustrate one of the major themes of this paper: discounting sources of the sensational stripe, or hearsay evidence, it is difficult to find positive information about the social adventures of the Chief Executive.

In final statement, in conclusion, the question of what effect a presidential sexual life has upon national politics is hard to answer. I don't think it will ever be definitively answered. All I do tonight is to raise the question. Certainly Sigmund Freud and his disciples spoke of the sexual and the power drives, and this whole subject is something I want to think through a little more but it's exciting and even titillating to at least mention it.

I think two points need to be made. One I've repeated so often as to be like the woman in Shakespeare who protested too much. I cannot reiterate it too often, however, and that is that historians must be very, very careful when treading over territory that is known to be full of quicksand, and this is one of those subjects. The hard sources are not readily available. And yet, this fact notwithstanding, the subject deserves attention and study. Sexuality, like medical and health problems in general, is a complex and a dynamic influence which is very obvious, in fact so obvious as to be little realized and certainly seldom spoken of, and even more rarely committed to writing. And yet this factor undoubtedly helps shape personality and while impossible to measure with precision, must have had some effect on the course of presidential administrations.

2. Relevance: Does the Information Relate to the Topic?

In order to be able to answer this question correctly, you have to know how to recognize the topic. That takes some skill. Three common errors crop up in students' notes: keeping the topic too general, making the topic too specific, and combining two topics into one.

Let's look back at the example of "Overzealous" notes in Chapter 1. That note-taker was guilty of two of the errors. Her main topic, "Money and Interest," combined two separate topics into one—one of them a subtopic of the other. (The actual topic of the lecture was *interest*.) The first subtopic shown in the notes, "period, principal, interest, amount," was too specific. One word, "definitions," covers all these ideas and is much more descriptive of what the notes are about.

It's important to jot down the main topic of a lecture or reading assignment *before* you begin taking any notes. Otherwise you won't be able to know which ideas are relevant and which aren't. In another section of this chapter, we'll show how a course outline can help you recognize a topic the moment it's discussed. If you've got a book or lecturer that doesn't stick to easy-to-recognize topic development, you may start out with the wrong topic in your notes; be sure to correct it as soon as you can.

Some lecturers delight in entertaining with stories that have nothing to do with the topic. An instructor of Judi's gave daily reports on his progress in refinishing his home. Some authors like to parade dazzling but irrelevant facts and figures. It may be fascinating that Carl Sandburg's wife spent two years trying to get his first poem published, but it's irrelevant to the understanding of his poem *Chicago*. Clutter your notes with these irrelevancies, and you'll not only have to weed them out carefully later on (or else end up studying a lot of ideas you'll never be tested on), you may also miss noticing an important to-the-point statistic while you're rushing to copy down unneeded information.

Test your ability to catch what's irrelevant by crossing out the irrelevancies in the previous speech excerpt. (See Appendix B for the answers.) Then go through some of *your* notes checking specifically to see that no unwanted irrelevancies have crept in. If you find more than one or two, make special effort to keep this point in mind for the next several weeks. After a while, you'll no longer have to think about it consciously; it'll become second nature to sift out and take down only what's related to the topic at hand.

3. Importance: Do You Need the Information?

A detail can be true and relevant to a topic, yet still not be important enough to preserve in your notes. Let's say, for example, that in a book chapter whose topic is "Are Women More Emotional Than Men?" the following points are offered:

1. Women are quicker to respond to physical and mental stimuli.
2. Women bear pain better than men.
3. Unreliable nineteenth-century statistics show that fewer men than women were in mental homes.

Sentences 1 and 2 should be summed up in your notes: they're not only to the point, but important evidence for and against the point. Sentence 3, while certainly related to the topic, isn't worth copying because, by its own contention, the information is unreliable and therefore worthless.

Here are several common indicators of importance:

- *Truth:* If a statement isn't true, it isn't generally important *unless* it was (or is) believed by an important person or group of people.
- *Reliability:* If the source of a statement isn't reliable, the statement is generally unimportant.

- *Degree of detail:* If a true, reliable statement has to do with a detail so minor, you'll never be expected to remember it, it is—by definition—unimportant and therefore not worth jotting down.

As a test of your ability to decide what's important, go back to the speech we reprinted on pages 10–17 and jot down—as if you were taking notes for an exam—everything you believe to be important. Compare your answer to ours in Appendix B. (Save your notes so you can use them to complete the exercise on page 28 in Chapter 3.)

4. Personal Bias: Do You Want to Remember the Information?

Some people have great memories for dates and names; others have photographic memories for anything they see on the blackboard. Some of us can't remember much of anything unless we write it down. Obviously, your notes will reflect your personal memory skills. (That's one reason it's often disastrous for one person to rely on another person's notes.)

Sometimes an unimportant detail may strike you as a jumping-off point for further investigation, or as a colorful filler for a future exam or paper. In that case, by all means write it down—but also jot down the *reason* you're including it.

Sometimes information that's irrelevant for this project seems likely to be helpful for another one. If that's the case, put it down—but put it on another piece of paper, not the one having to do with this topic.

AIDS THAT PUT YOUR NOTES IN PERSPECTIVE

Scientists have taught monkeys how to type—but they still can't teach them to type long letters home. Scientists may some day teach monkeys how to take dictation—but we bet that if they're tested on those notes, they'll flunk. If you copy notes automatically, without understanding the words or their relationship to the rest of the course, you'll do as well as a monkey on your next test.

To ensure that each day's notes make sense and fit into the big picture of the entire course, prepare for each course as follows:

1. Buy, Borrow, or Make a Course Outline

A course outline is the best aid to understanding where a particular lecture or reading fits into the course as a whole. Buy, borrow, or make one—and keep it permanently inserted at the beginning of your course notes. In some schools, outlines are for sale by the Student Union, a copy center, or some other enterprising group. (Some booklets that are sold as lecture notes are really heavily overwritten course outlines.) Some professors distribute course outlines the first day of class. If you can't locate a course outline, make your own with guidance from a friend's course notes or from the units and chapter titles in your textbook. The outline may not end up entirely up to date, accurate, or in the correct sequence, but it will give you a general picture of what you're expected to get out of the course.

If you're taking your outline from a book's table of contents, don't just read it; *copy it* on paper in your own words. For one thing, your mind will do more thinking, understanding, and remembering when you write. For another, you'll begin to notice and decode some of the course jargon. Besides, you'll need a convenient copy of that outline to refer to during the rest of the course.

For English, Psych, or Social Studies, you may have many assigned readings. In that case, list each reading's title and topic. Then, like a detective, find the threads that tie the readings together. Is the *perspective* current or historical? Is the *focus* global or geographically narrow? Is there a *bias* in favor of one point of view, or are several contradictory viewpoints included? You should be able to answer these and other pertinent questions just by quickly skimming the assigned materials. Again, do it in writing—and then turn it into a course outline.

Your course outline should answer at least the following questions. You can use our outline as a template.

1. Course title
   A. Main topic
      a. 1st subtopic
      b. 2nd subtopic
      [*etc.*]
   B. Next main topic
      a. 1st subtopic
      [*etc.*]
   C. [*etc.*]

To check your understanding of course outlines, pretena that this book is the only textbook assigned for a course that's listed in the catalog as "Methods of Note-Taking." Take 10 minutes to prepare a course outline. Our outline is in Appendix C.

2. Start Learning the Course Jargon

Every course has its special vocabulary and catch phrases. New words are introduced (like *byte* in computer language); old words take on new meanings (like *specific* in the term *specific gravity*); some word groups get repeated over and over again (like *primary support group* in psychology). Your note-taking will go a lot faster if you begin the course prepared to learn its jargon just as you begin German prepared to learn *its* new language.

1. Buy a pack of 3 × 5 index cards. Then begin to use them systematically. Whenever you hear or read an unfamiliar term, jot it down quickly. As soon as you have a

minute, define each new term accurately on the other side of its card. Keep the cards in alphabetical order and check, every once in a while, to make sure you know the meanings of all these new words.

2. If the course involves formulas you have to be able to find quickly, begin to jot each new formula (with its application or derivation) on a 3 × 5 card. In some courses, formulas are part of the basic vocabulary, and your card pack can be grabbed at a moment's notice and studied on a bus. (If the course has just one assigned textbook, also try this timesaver: tape a sheet of paper inside the front or back cover, and on it keep an up-to-date list of important formulas and the page numbers that show their derivations.)

3. Begin a list or card file of jargon words and phrases— the ones that keep cropping up all the time. Devise shorthand ways of writing these words and phrases, and note these shorthand cues on your list. That way, you'll be able to decipher a cue if you forget what its shorthand was meant to stand for. "Primary support group," for example, could become, in shorthand, p-s-gp. Your definition card would then read *primary support group (p-s-gp)*.

Students tend to treat each lecture and each reading assignment as an isolated fragment, never relating it to the rest of the readings and lectures in the course. The rare student who does make all the connections is the one who walks away with As. If you keep a course outline handy, and check at the beginning of each reading assignment or lecture to see where it fits into the outline, making those important connections will soon become second nature.

Students also tend to try to escape learning the course jargon. They skim over unknown words, or grab at approximate meanings. The students who make those words part of their vocabularies are the ones who spout them back easily on exams and papers. Using the jargon signals, "I can pitch in your league."

3

How to Organize Notes

Try this experiment: See how quickly you can memorize the following number:

0026006246810

Did you divide the number into three sets, and note that the second set (0062) is the first set (0026) with the last two numbers inverted and that the third set (46810) is made up of the first 4 even numbers that follow the "2" at the end of the previous set (4-6-8-10)?

If you did—or found some other pattern for remembering—you proved the main point in this chapter: People's minds remember best when they make patterns out of what they hear or read. To remember your coursework, you should be forming the information into patterns.

Often, it's easy to make those patterns. Good books and good lecturers deliver their information in well-patterned blocks. But some texts—and some instructors—are completely disorganized. You have to find the pattern that ties together what you're reading or hearing. The best preparation for being able to get an A despite a poor textbook or badly organized professor is lots of practice in taking organized notes.

In the early grades, your teachers did all your organizing for you. The first day of school you were not only told to buy pencils, pens, rulers, and notebooks; you were often told precisely what kind of notebook to buy. When you arrived the second day—with your notebook—you were instructed on how it should be set up. Different teachers preferred different systems, but all of them wanted you to keep your subjects separate. Somewhere along the way, if you were lucky, you had a teacher who insisted that you outline your notes.

Many students rebel against these teacher-imposed note-taking systems the first chance they get. If the rebellion occurs in high school, they're lucky: lowered grades soon convince the smart ones that some system is needed. The fact is, information sinks in best if notes are organized.

HOW TO USE OUTLINE FORM

As we pointed out in Chapter 2, ideas fall into two general categories: fact and opinion. Facts themselves can generally be put into the following hierarchy of importance:

A. Main idea
  1. subtopic
    a. support

The Main Idea

The main idea is a broad topic or a general rule—a kind of file-folder label that ties together many bits of related information. A good lecturer or chapter presents the main idea first, and labels it clearly so you can't miss it. If a book or lecture is disorganized, the main idea may become apparent only after you've taken notes on all its bits and pieces.

It's possible—though not usual—for one lecture or chapter to have several main ideas, or for one main idea to be covered in several lectures or chapters. In a textbook, a chapter's title usually spells out its main idea. (Note this book's chapter titles.)

Subtopics or Subordinate Topics

Subordinate topics or subtopics are the various pieces that fit together to form the main idea. These, too, are often file-folder kinds of categories, just subdivisions like rooms in a house. They are either *components* of the topic, or answer a question about the topic: what, why, where, when, how, or who.

One example of subtopics is the "Just Right" notes in Chapter 1. The two subordinate topics are "Simple interest" and "Compound interest." For another example, see our three main subheadings in Chapter 1. Notice that they answer the question *why* about the main topic "take good notes" which is mentioned in the chapter's title. Sometimes broad or complicated subtopics are further broken down into sub-subtopics, which are then organized individually. For an example, notice how our subtopic "Facts" in Chapter 2 is further divided. (See pages 8–9).

Supporting Statements

Supports are the definitions, explanations, examples, opinions, and proofs that bolster all the subordinate topics. To see how they're used, refer to the evidence cited in Appendix B.

In lectures and textbooks (but not always in fiction), *opinion* is rarely a main topic or even a subtopic. Usually it's used as a support to a factual idea and belongs in that part of your organization. In the main, details—statistics, anecdotes, quotations, proofs for all general statements—belong in this third level of outline organization. But sometimes—particularly in math and the sciences—definitions do form subordinate topics of their own.

Don't confuse level of *hierarchy* in your outline's organization for *level of importance* in a paper or on an exam. Few general statements (which you'd put into the first level of organization in your outline) are worth much unless they're backed up by several pieces of supporting evidence or evaluating quotation (which you'd put into the second or third level in your outline's organization). Few broad ideas are convincing on their own; they become convincing when supported by the details and specifics that belong in the third level of your outline. Few rules hold water without examples that prove them. Likewise, your own notes are not complete unless they include a great deal of third-level specifics.

As you can see, the pattern of organization we've just described is the classic Outline Form we hope some early-grades teacher explained to you. If you recall, it looked something like this in your notes:

A.
  1.
      a.
      b.
      c.
  2.
      a.
      b.
B.
  1.
      [*etc.*]

Exercise

Test your ability to use Outline Form by organizing into a structure just like that shown on page 27, the notes that you made on the speech in Chapter 2. Then compare your results with ours in Appendix D.

HOW TO WORK OUTLINE FORM INTO A MEMORY CLUE SYSTEM

Quite a bit of research has been done on note-taking organization, and until recently one system was considered best for everyone. It's the *Memory Clue* system of note-taking. If you don't have a system of your own that works well, begin with this one.

A. Use a binder that contains approximately 8½″ × 11″ looseleaf paper, and write on *just one side.* This may seem wasteful, but it's one time when you shouldn't cut corners.

B. Write the words *Main Topic* on line 1 of each page.

C. Rule each page as follows:

   1. If the course is one in which lecture and text are closely related, use the 2-3-3-2 technique. Make columns of two inches down the left-hand side for memory clues (which we'll explain very soon), three inches in the middle for lecture notes, and three inches on the right side for textbook notes. Leave a two-inch space across the bottom of each page for your own observations and conclusions.

   Each notebook page for the course should look like the sample shown on page 29.

   2. If it's a course where the lectures and the readings are not closely related, use separate pages for reading notes and class notes, following the 2-5-1 technique: two inches at left for memory clues, five

PAGE RULED FOR TEXTBOOK *AND* LECTURE NOTES

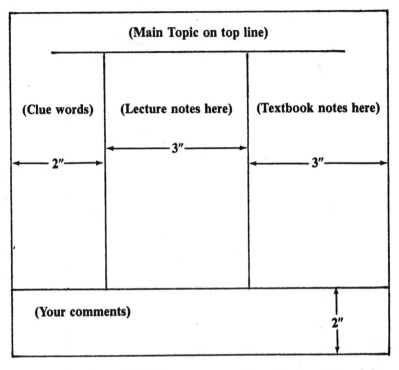

in the middle for notes, and an inch at the right for your own observations and impressions. (After a while you won't need to draw actual lines.)

Each notebook page for that course should look like the sample shown on page 30.

The *Memory Clue* column is the big plus in this system. In this column, after you've taken all your notes, you'll set down clue words that'll help you find facts at a glance and study for exams. The clue words don't repeat information, but label or pinpoint what you'll need to remember. They're the kind of clues you would put on crib sheets. For example, to help you remember the information contained

PAGE RULED FOR LECTURE *OR* TEXTBOOK NOTES

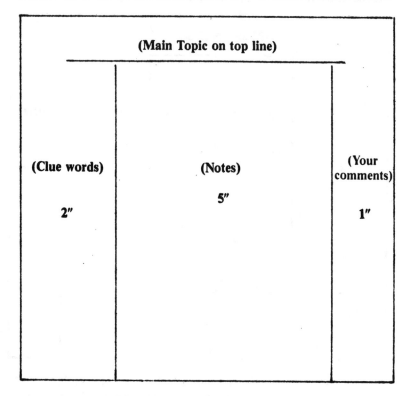

so far here in Tip 1, your clue column would look like this:

> binder, 8½ × 11 looseleaf
> 1 side
> top: Main Topic
> 2-3-3-2
> 2-5-1
> L-h col = clue wds

To test your understanding of how to write Memory Clues, turn to the notes you made for the speech in Chapter 1. Jot down the clues you'd need to remember these points. Compare your clues with ours shown in Appendix E.

The advantage of the Memory Clue note-taking system is that it makes you think about your notes after you take them, helping you to make sense of them and remember them. It's a sure guarantee of higher grades.

HOW TO USE PATTERNING TO ORGANIZE NOTES

There's a new kind of note-taking that works well for experienced note-takers who can pick out words easily, and for people who enjoy mathematical games. If you learn best through visual recall (remembering what you *see*), learning this method will pay off in big dividends. It works best when you're dealing with ideas, as in the social sciences, or with things that divide into smaller and smaller parts. For example, the parts of a cell, the members of the animal kingdom, and an analysis of Freud's theories all lend themselves to this kind of note-taking. It works like this:

Within a circle, square, star, or any other pattern that whimsy suggests so long as it's approximately centered on your note-page, print the main topic of the lecture or book selection. Then draw lines out from the topic to rest the subtopics on. (Printing is an important part of this system, so don't scrawl in longhand.) Supporting evidence or examples branch off from the subtopics. They include all those who-what-where-when-why-how answers.

On page 32, you'll find our pattern for notes on the topic "Systematize Your Note-Taking with OK4R," which will be discussed fully in Chapter 5.

A variation of patterning, the *pyramid,* works well in showing a main topic that includes a number of lesser ideas. Our illustration of a pyramid on page 33 shows two ways of designing yours—one way (the left side), being more free-form than the other.

You can make other kinds of patterns, too. For example,

A Pattern for Remembering OK4R

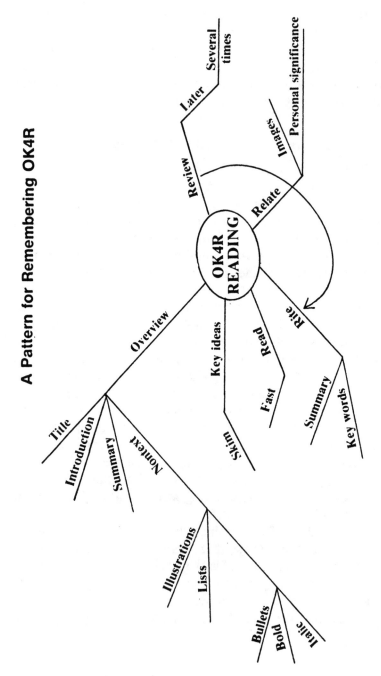

A Pyramid for Remembering OK4R

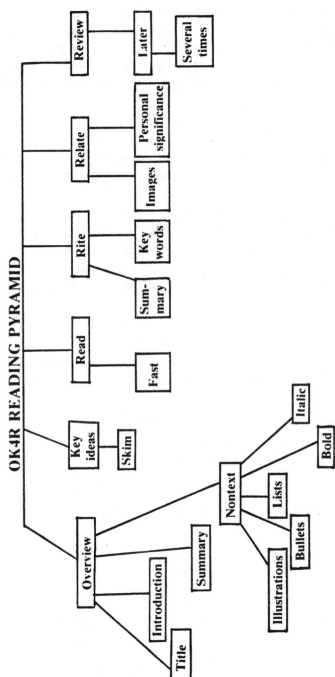

OK4R READING PYRAMID

chronological information fits best on a time-line pattern (page 34). Comparative information is most clearly shown on a graph (page 34) or a flow chart (page 35). Parts of a whole can be drawn on a pie graph (page 35). Once you have the hang of patterning, you'll find you can write less and remember more.

TIME LINE: HUMAN RIGHTS

1776	US: Declaration of Independence
1789	France: Declaration of Rights of Man and the Citizen
1791	US: Bill of Rights
1810–25	Most of Latin America: independence from Spain
1832	England: Great Reform Bill
1848	France, Austria, Italy, Prussia: revolutions
1861	Czar emancipates serfs, Russia; U.S. abolishes slavery
1917	Russia: revolution
1920	US: women get vote
1947	Asia & Africa: European colonies get independence
1948	UN: Universal Declaration of Human Rights

GRAPH: DEATH RATE IN LONDON DURING BLACK PLAGUE

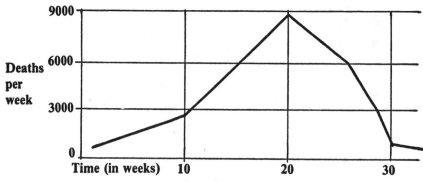

FLOW CHART: SYSTEM FOR FINDING AVERAGE IQ

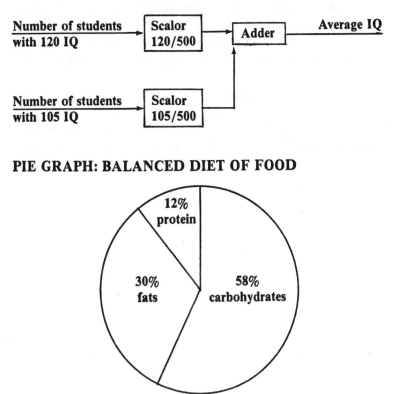

PIE GRAPH: BALANCED DIET OF FOOD

Patterning has many advantages over traditional outline-form note-taking:

1. You have to think and organize *before* you write. You can't just passively copy from a book or lecture. That in itself helps you remember twice as much as before.
2. The main topic, and the links between ideas, are shown clearly for later study. (Notice the arrow in the OK4R pattern.)
3. Because patterning is so graphic, you remember your notes longer.

4. No two patterns look alike. This, too, helps memory.
5. You can add new information easily where it belongs, even if your book or lecturer skips around.
6. You can become creative in forming the patterns, turning note-taking from a drag to a challenge.

If you've never done any patterned note-taking, we suggest you begin slowly, with easy-to-pattern subjects and with book chapters instead of lectures. Shift to lecture patterning only when thinking about the patterns won't interfere with your concentration on what's being said.

4

Shortcuts for Note-Taking

Taking good notes is hard work: it involves brain strain and pen-pushing. To make it less of a chore, we hope that by now you've devised your own system of note-taking shortcuts. If not, begin today, adding one or two new shorthand symbols and abbreviations each week. (Don't try for too many at once or you'll end up with a set of hieroglyphics you can't read and can't remember.)

USE OF SHORTHAND FOR QUICKER NOTE-TAKING

Speedwriting books have lots of ideas you can borrow quickly. So do the sciences. Here are some shortcuts we find especially helpful; let them help you get started.

1. Leave out all periods from abbreviations.

2. Borrow technical symbols.

&	and
+	and, plus, positive
−	minus, negative
÷	divided (by)
×	times, multiplied by
=	equals, is the same as
≠	doesn't equal, is not the same as
≅	is approximately equal to, is similar
<	(is) less than, is increasing to
>	(is) more than, is decreasing to
→	approaches, approaching, to the end
∝	varies, varying, varied
∠	angle
⊥	perpendicular, is perpendicular to
‖	parallel, is parallel to
f	frequency, frequent, frequently
/	ratio, ratio of (for example, height/weight = the ratio of height to weight)
%	percent, percentage
#	number
$	dollars
¢	cents
( )	parenthetical
∧	insert, insertion
@	amount, the amount of, at
?	question, the question is
!	here's a surprising fact

3. Use standard abbreviations from Engl and other langs.

cf	compare	sub	subordinate
eg	for example	subj	subject
c/o	care of	ca	approximately
lb	pound	ng	no good
H_2O	water	dept	department
min	minimum	etc	and so forth
max	maximum		

4. Make up your own abbreviations for common words and letter sets, but be careful that your abbreviations can't be mistaken, in context, for other words. (In other words, *soc* would be a fine abbreviation for society, but are you sure you might not mistake it for sociology or social?)
   a. Eliminate vowels

-mt	-ment
-tn	-tion
pblm	problem
gvt	government
indvl	individual
dvlp	develop
bkgd	background
mxtr	mixture

   b. Use word beginnings

assoc	associate
intro	introduction
info	information
bio	biography, biographical
biol	biology
mil	military, militant
com	committee
comm	commission
mixt	mixture
rep	representative

5. Add "s" to abbreviations or symbols to show plural.

+s	plusses, advantages
cfs	comparisons
govts	governments

Usually, the longer the original word, the more easily its abbreviation will be recognized; the shorter the word, the easier it will be to read back if you leave in its vowels. Keep in mind that the purpose of your shorthand is to make note-taking quicker and easier without giving up easy readability. If it takes more time to remember a symbol than to write out the word, forget the symbol. Be sure to build your system patiently, a few symbols and abbreviations each week.

Exercise

Practice some of the above shorthand suggestions by copying the speech passage "Eros in the White House" that's excerpted in Chapter 2.

Next test your note-taking and shorthand skills by turning to the beginning of this chapter. Take just five minutes to make quick notes on its contents. Then compare your notes with ours in Appendix F.

5

Taking Notes from Assigned Text

Almost every course you take in school has some kind of assigned textbook. The course instructor assumes that this required background reading gives every student an identical basic knowledge and perspective on the subject to build on in the lectures and to be tested on in the exams.

In high school, teachers often teach to the lowest common denominator. They figure that most students are slow or lazy, so they review much of the assigned text in class. If you're a bright student, you may have been able to slip through by just listening in class and never cracking a book. But in college, most instructors not only aim their courses at the bright students, but expect those students to be thoroughly prepared for lectures and exams. The assigned background reading should not only be done when assigned, but careful notes should be taken as you go along. And you must use a special kind of reading skill.

LEARN HOW TO READ FOR A COURSE

When you're reading for your own personal pleasure, whether it's a sci-fi novel or a book on improving your tennis stroke, you can zip through it skipping the dull parts. If you later don't understand something because of what you skipped, or don't remember a fact because you skimmed quickly, nobody but you will know or care.

But you don't have that luxury when you're reading for a course. You're responsible for knowing what's in the dull parts as well as the lively ones. You're expected to remember all the important details.

Most students find their assigned reading overwhelming because nobody's taught them that it should be read differently from reading for pleasure. You can't just read through from beginning to end. You have to know how and when to skim. And in order to take good notes, you must know what to look for, whether skimming or reading every word.

1. How to Skim

The word *skim* describes the same process that gets us *skim milk,* and if you think of it that way, skimming will become easy. To skim milk, the cream is taken off the top. To skim a reading, we lift off what's important from all the words that are floating on a page.

Obviously, nobody can skim effectively unless he can recognize what is important. If you are still having trouble, reread Chapter 2. In addition, here are a few general guidelines to help you.

• To skim well, push your eye along so that it takes in large blocks of words. In general, ignore everything but the nouns and verbs. Skimming is really no different from speed reading, except that skimming is a searching-out operation. Its three components are: (a) rapid reading; (b) unwandering attention; and (c) keeping in mind what you're looking for.

- Some authors make skimming a snap because they're fine organizers. They insert subheads as flags to tell you their topics. They put important ideas in **bold** or *italics*. They always begin their paragraphs with summarizing sentences. If your book seems carefully organized, watch for these skimming aids.
- It's almost impossible to skim good fiction. The better the author, the more cleverly she hides important plot development and characterization. To catch all the clues, you must read nearly every word. It's true that some authors go on for pages describing a sunrise; you can skip the passage if sunrises don't turn you on (and you're relatively certain the instructor won't test your recall of Faulkner's sunset scene)—but only if you skim by reading quickly to make sure that no important message is hidden in the description.

HOW TO TAKE NOTES FROM FICTION

Fiction—a play, short story, or novel—is generally assigned reading just in literature courses. But not always; for example, a history professor might assign *A Tale of Two Cities* as background for lectures on the French Revolution. In reading fiction for any course, make sure your notes include the following information.

A. Author's Name, Title of Work

This information should be carefully written, correctly spelled, at the top of your first page of notes—where the main topic would go in nonfiction outlining—and belongs in abbreviated form at the top of every page after that.

B. Year the Work Was Written

In most cases, this can be approximated—but it's important to know when the author wrote so that you can understand the climate of thought that influenced him.

C. Author's Nationality and (If Different) the Country in Which the Work Was Written

Note these for the same reason given for B.

D. Reason for Inclusion

Put down, in your notes, the reason (or reasons) you think your instructor assigned the reading you're about to do. Is the author considered great? If so, what's her claim to fame: her use of dialogue? her story-telling ability? her innovative style? or what? As an example of what we mean, reread the reason we suggested just above for including *A Tale of Two Cities* in a history course's assigned reading list.

As you read, keep your eye out for examples that illustrate the reasons you've been assigned the selection. They belong in your notes, because they're almost sure to be on an exam.

E. Names and Distinguishing Characteristics of the Main Characters

The main characters are the ones that are vital to the story. Erase a main character, and the story is incapable of happening the way the author has described it. Name your main characters and tell enough about each one to bring a picture clearly to mind half a year from now.

F. Theme of the Story

Most story themes can be told in a sentence or two. In *The Wizard of Oz,* for example, the theme is a young girl's search for the way home. Don't confuse the author's theme with your instructor's reasons for having you read the work; they're rarely the same. (In this case, the reasons might be to illustrate the influence of early twentieth-century morality on American literature.) And don't confuse theme with plot. In the latter, you'd incorporate the struggle by good Dorothy and the naive Munchkins against the Wicked Witch.

G. Plot of the Story

This can almost *never* be told in a sentence. It's a summary of the *action* that takes place in the story. You needn't put in every detail, but every important scene should be mentioned. If you've got a good memory, your plot outline can be sketchy, but do fill in as much as you need to recall the story line six months from now.

H. New Thoughts or Insights Suggested to You by the Assigned Reading

This may be the most important part of your notes. If you write down your ideas right after finishing the assignment, you'll remember them for the next essay or exam question. If you don't write them down—no matter how clever they seem to you at the time—you'll probably forget them once you go on to the next project.

Obviously, some of the above information can be written down before you begin the assigned reading, and some will have to wait until you're finished. If the selection has an introduction, don't skip it no matter how sorely you're tempted. Skim it: it probably fills in much of the important information that we've just suggested you get. (We can often separate the C students from the B students simply by asking whether they're in the habit of skipping book introductions.)

HOW TO TAKE TEXTBOOK NOTES

Assigned nonfiction falls into two categories: the textbook and the book written for a general audience. The textbook is often the hub of a course, its key component, so it's important to learn how to read it so that you can take good notes.

Textbooks are generally assigned chapter by chapter and in college the assignments are often made in bulk at the beginning of the course. There's no benevolent *in locus parentis* to remind you at week six to read week six's chapter assignment. If you get behind, you may have to struggle to follow along in the lectures. So the first rule of textbook reading is *don't get behind*.

Few instructors cover everything that's in the assigned textbook, but most of them hold you responsible for remembering it all on exams. The better your notes, the better you'll be able to study for tests.

1. Size Up the Textbook

Before you begin Chapter 1, find out what's in the book. How good is its table of contents? Does it have an index? Are there special sections at the end of the book with quiz answers, formula charts, log and function tables? Skim the introduction. It often contains useful suggestions, and sometimes important warnings as well.

Page through the book. See how it's arranged. It'll make your chapter-by-chapter reading go faster.

Decide now on the note-taking method you want to use for the course: outline, patterning, or a combination of the two. Are you combining book notes with lecture notes or keeping them separate? Set up your notebook accordingly.

When you begin your first reading assignment—and for every assignment after that—keep your notebook nearby.

2. Systematize Your Note-Taking with OK4R

To keep your textbook notes in sharp focus, researchers have developed a number of systems with catchy names like SQ3R, OK4R, PANORAMA, REAP, OARWET, and PQRST. They've all been proven to work if you stick with them. Here's our own modification of the one we prefer, the OK4R system developed by educator Dr. Walter Pauk. (It's the system we outlined in pattern form in Chapter 3.)

O. *Overview:* Before you begin reading a chapter from start to finish, get a bird's-eye view of it. Read its title and any summarizing words that the author put between title and chapter beginning. Read the chapter's first and last paragraphs; often they summarize all the main points in the chapter. In some textbooks, the chapter begins or ends with a paragraph actually headed *summary* or its Latin synonym *precis.*

At the top of your notes write down the main topic. But don't write any more until you've finished reading the chapter. For now, put your notebook aside.

Next, still for an overview, read all the headings in the chapter: the words in italics, bold type, or larger print. Glance through all the bulleted (•) sections and all the itemizations that stand out on the page. As you go along, look at pictures, graphs, and tables: all the illustrative material. Read the captions so you know what they represent. You'll end up with a very clear idea of what the chapter is about. In fact, in many textbooks, the words between the headings and illustrations are just the third-string details; the stand-out type tells all the main ideas.

K. *Key ideas:* Now, still without taking notes, *skim* the text for its key ideas. (We'd like to call this part *S* because *s*kimming for *s*ubtopics is what's important, but OK4R is easier to remember than OS4R.) What Dr. Pauk calls a "key idea" is the same as what we called a "subtopic" in our chapter on outlining. In a well-organized textbook, you'll find the key ideas in the chapter subheadings. But not all textbooks are well organized.

R1. *Read* your assignment from beginning to end. *Do it quickly.* You'll be able to because you already know where the author is headed and what he's trying to show. Don't slow up or you'll start thinking about other things and all your reading will result in just a big hole in your memory.

R2. *Rite:* Now it's time to write in your notebook. You'll remember better if you can do it with your textbook closed, but if you need reminders keep it open. Using whatever note-taking method you've decided on, write down all the subtopics in order, and the details or examples that the author used to illustrate each point. Try for at least three details for every subtopic. (Sometimes subtopics are broken up into several sub-subtopics before the details are given. Where that's been done, stick to the author's organization. Your outline form will show an extra level of hierarchy. Instead of being organized A, 1, a, it'll be A, 1, a, I or I, A, 1, a.)

Don't try to shortcut by simply copying down subheadings or by taking notes only on the author's summary. Summaries contain none of the details that you'll need for an exam. And sometimes book publishers stick in extraneous subheadings to make a page look jazzy or to break up large blocks of text.

R3. *Relate:* Think about your notes. Relate them to the last several chapters and lectures and to the course outline. Put them in perspective. If it's a lecturer's style to go over textbook information, be prepared to note where she disagrees with the book and where she presents information that's more up-to-date.

R4. *Review:* This step should not take place right away. It should be saved for the next short quiz, and then again for later tests throughout the term. It seems self-evident to us that notes are taken with the purpose of being reviewed for exams—but we've discovered that some students never reread them until just before finals. That's akin to preparing a gourmet meal and letting it sit for six months before eating it—by that time, it's all so stale you might as well forget it and start all over again.

HOW TO TAKE NOTES ON NONTEXTBOOK NONFICTION

For nontextbook nonfiction—journal articles, essays, source materials, and books written for general audiences—the following four-step procedure is our favorite. To remember it, think SRQR.

S. *Skim:* Skim through the pages of the assigned material, reading whatever catches your eye: titles, subheads, italicized phrases, lists, illustrations. If you find any summaries, read them through—but do it *after* you've skimmed all the pages.

R. *Read:* Read the whole selection *quickly,* penciling check marks next to important parts and question marks next to parts that you can't understand. Underline phrases only if you're *sure* they contain key ideas. Don't stop now to try to figure out anything. That comes later. Don't stop to take notes either.

Q. *Question:* Now go back to the parts you've questioned, and figure out what they mean. You'll find you'll understand these sections better now that you've seen some of the thinking that comes afterward. Often, an author rephrases difficult ideas many times in a chapter, and the second or third time his wording makes more sense.

R. *Rite:* Now's the time to take notes on what you've read, using the check marks as helpful guideposts. Be sure to organize your notes, jotting down the main topic first and then the subtopics. Put in the significant details that back up the author's conclusions and observations, either in outline form or with patterning.

Here, too, as with all note-taking, *review* is an important part of the process.

LEARN HOW TO WRITE IN YOUR BOOKS

One of the many popular systems for note-taking suggests underlining your school books in four or five different shades of ink. One shade is for topics, another for examples, still another for names or dates to be memorized. We've seen this system fall apart more than once simply because the four-color pen was lost. We've seen students devote more attention to finding the right color than to making sense of what they were reading. In addition, there's another drawback: some bookstores won't buy back heavily underlined books. (For good reasons, too. If you're the kind of student who shops for pre-underlined books, have you ever thought that maybe the underliner missed the book's point and ended up with a D in the course?)

But we do advocate making some marks in your books (in pencil so they can be erased, and never in library books). Here are our suggestions.

1. Use the Margins—Sparingly

Read nonfiction with a pencil in hand. For one thing, it helps you stay awake. For another, you can make a few marks in the margins as you go along. It's best if you devise your own system: you'll remember it easier. But here are a few suggestions to get you started.

- *?:* for anything you don't understand or want to come

back to and reread. (If you still don't understand it on rereading, leave in the *?* and make a note at the top of your next lecture-notes page to ask about it in class.)

- √: for anything that probably should go into your notes. (But don't stop now and take the notes. After you finish the reading, you may change your ideas about what you need notes on.)

- *subheads:* if the book isn't broken up with topic subheads, put your own in the margins so you can find information at a glance. Keep your subheads sparse— no more than two to a page.

- *circled words:* do this to words you don't understand and will want to look up later when you're taking notes—unless you've been able to figure them out from explanations further on in the reading.

- *your own thoughts, conclusions, or specific questions:* jot these briefly in the margins as they pop into your head while you're reading, so that you won't forget them when you're done.

2. Note Significant Pages on the Front Inside Cover

This system works particularly well for nonfiction that isn't written in textbook fashion. To mark important ideas so you can find them again, in addition to a check in the page margin, note the page number and—in brief—the topic in pencil on the front inside cover of the book. (If the book is borrowed, clip a piece of paper onto the title page.) Here's what the inside cover of our copy of *Walden* looks like:

12—what's necessary	53–4—costs
14—who book is for	61—auctions
19—clothing conventions	64—against reg. houses (219 too)
28—civilized vs savage	79—astronomy
36—building his house	

Below this list, which actually continues with 10 more citations, is the following:

?—42, 69, 70, 73, 79, 80, 131, 143
good quotes—29, 33, 63, 82, 100, 174, 288

This data was written more than 20 years ago, and it still summarizes the book for us today.

3. Put Important Data at the End of the Book

Some authors list important definitions, equivalents, formulas, and other data at the back of the book. If your book doesn't have what you need for easy reference, you can start an index that gives formulas and meanings, as well as page numbers on which they're derived; or that shows basic concepts and notes the pages on which they're defined.

You can tip in your own equivalents tables, and your own list of standard abbreviations. These back-of-the-book references will not only save time when you're doing homework, they'll be valuable aids for open-book or take-home exams.

A WORD ABOUT OTHER NOTE-TAKING SYSTEMS

As we've said before, there are many systems for taking notes on assigned reading. Some of them have overwhelming drawbacks. One system suggests that before you begin an assignment, you figure out questions to ask yourself while you're reading. But if you don't have any background on a topic, finding questions takes more time than it's worth.

Some systems advise you to read the first sentence of every paragraph before you read through the entire selection. But few authors consciously remember to put a paragraph's topic in the first sentence. Sometimes it's there;

often it isn't. Skimming the entire passage quickly is generally just as effective—and it's predictably useful for any kind of author.

If you're using one of these systems—or one of your own devising—and it works for you, don't change just for the sake of change. But if you have no system of note-taking for assigned reading, try the ones we've outlined in this chapter. When it comes to taking good notes, *system* is a basic ingredient.

There's not enough space here to reprint a whole chapter from another book in order to test how systematic you've become. We suggest that you get your practice by plunging in for real. Begin now to take systematic notes on all your assignments. We guarantee that, as you practice, it'll become easier and easier.

6

Taking Lecture Notes

LISTENING VS. READING

Taking good notes while you're reading is child's play compared to the challenge of taking good lecture notes. You must not only be able to recognize what's noteworthy and to organize it well, but you must have these skills so ingrained that you don't have to think about them consciously. All your conscious attention must focus on the lecturer's words and actions, and you must be able to keep pace with them. Unlike the printed page, the lecturer rarely gives you a second opportunity to make sense of what he's saying.

We'll assume that you didn't spring full-blown into this world yesterday, but that you've been getting by—however badly—with some kind of lecture-note system. We urge you to stay with *that* system when you're taking your lecture notes until you're completely comfortable with this book's system. Once you are, reread the previous pages to make sure that you've got it all down pat. Only then do we suggest that you begin using this chapter's guidelines.

Exercise

Here's a short quiz to help you decide whether you're ready for this chapter. If you are ready, the quiz will be simply a five-minute review. But if you're not, it ought to point out valuable tips you've missed in earlier chapters.

1. What are the four criteria for deciding whether something's worth putting down in your notes?
2. What are the two main divisions of information?
3. What are the three kinds of facts, and which of these kinds need evidence behind them?
4. Name the three most common kinds of evidence.
5. Name three common indicators of a subject's importance.
6. What's an easy way to learn course jargon and formulas?
7. Set up an outline form, showing what kind of information belongs on each level.
8. Show two ways to set up your notebook if you're using the Memory Clue note-taking system, and tell when you'd use each one.
9. What is a Memory Clue?
10. Tell what patterning is, and name four kinds of note-taking patterns.
11. Name five different kinds of note-taking shortcuts.
12. Name the eight pieces of information that fiction notes should include.
13. What's the first thing to do when you're taking textbook notes?
14. Tell what OK4R stands for, and explain what each component word means.
15. Name and explain the steps in four-step nontextbook note-taking.

(The questions in the quiz are arranged in the order in which they're answered in the book. To check your answers, skim chapters 1 through 5.)

Are you sure you're ready? Then read on.

ORGANIZE YOUR TOOLS

The quickest way to sabotage your lecture notes is to neglect to plan ahead to have the right tools. You can lose many minutes' worth of important data while you're borrowing a pen or waiting for someone else's ruler. Invest in one of those plastic zippered carriers that snap into loose-leaf notebooks, and begin to fill it before the first lecture. In it keep two working pens at all times, and a pencil (with a good eraser) as well. A six-inch ruler is also a near-must, since even Social Studies sometimes calls for drawing graphs and time-lines. Use *duplicate* tools, not these, for your homework; otherwise you're sure to forget to put them back into your school pack on the most important day of the year.

Into the case, also put everything else you need for classes as soon as you find out you need them: compass, pocket calculator, templates, whatever your courses require. When you buy these things, buy two of each and keep one in your study desk. That way, if you lose or break the one in your pack, you can replace it fast. (Make sure you resupply your study desk drawer as soon as you can.)

As we've said before, leave your tape recorder home. The only time we can conceive of a tape recorder coming in handy is if you need to take notes in a pitch-dark room.

KEEP YOUR COURSE OUTLINE HANDY

Most students' lecture notes look like they were taken on a series of space shuttle missions. One day's notes rarely relate to the day before's or the next day's. They seem completely out of touch with one another, isolated fragments instead of a cohesive unit of thought.

That misses the whole point of taking a course, which is by definition *a cohesive unit.* The better you can tie together the lectures, the higher will be your grade.

Way back near the beginning, we suggested that you buy, borrow, or make a course outline before you get to the first lecture, and that you keep the outline on page 1 of your course notes. Used correctly, the course outline will tie together all your lecture notes. Here's how to use it: Each time you get to class, glance at the outline and mark the topic that was covered in the previous lecture. This will give you a one-minute review of what's been covered so far, and will automatically put today's topic in perspective.

KEEP YOUR MIND FROM WANDERING

The hardest job you'll ever have in any lecture class is keeping your full attention on the lecturer. Most instructors talk about ten times as slowly as students take notes. That's nine minutes of possible drift time for every minute of alertness—and once you drift you may miss the next important fact. Even if your professor's a four-star entertainer, your mind is apt to wander. (Beware the entertainers; they're usually the poorest organizers. And don't let your enjoyment keep you from catching that small vital fact snuck in between chuckles—it's sure to appear on the next exam.)

Several safeguards will keep your mind from wandering.

1. Choose a Seat Carefully

If you can select your own seat, choose it in the first or second row, away from tempting windows, under a good light, and near the center so you can see both ends of the blackboard. These seats are usually easy to come by, since most students foolishly shy away from them, not realizing that they're the least expensive way to guarantee a higher grade. (If you know that an overhead projector will be used, the second row is often better than the first.) You may not enjoy the feeling of being exposed to teacher's watchful eye, but it's that feeling that'll keep you from snoozing or gazing off into the distance. And if the lecturer is a mumbler, you're that much ahead if you're nearby.

If your lecturer likes to assign seats alphabetically and your name begins with T, fudge a little if you have to but give him a reason why you must sit front and center. Eyestrain, hearing problems, or just difficulty concentrating are all reasons most instructors respect.

2. Avoid Friends

Don't sit next to a friend unless she's a grind—or next to someone whom you're dying to date. The person in the next seat may become a friend by the time the course is over, but don't handicap yourself by starting out with someone who's bound to take your attention away from what's happening at the front of the room. (About that datable classmate: try tripping over him or her when you're leaving the classroom.)

3. Keep Lecture and Personal Matters Separate

Keep a personal notebook, or personal section of your looseleaf, specifically for extraneous notes. That way, if you suddenly remember that you need to get cash or do the laundry, you can quickly turn to the appropriate page and write down the thought. If you don't write it down, it'll continue to nag while you're trying to concentrate on the lecture. Get it off your mind and down onto paper—*not* the paper you're taking notes on—and you'll be able to get your mind back on what's happening in class.

This is a good time to remind you not to pass notes, try

for clever asides, or do any of those other cute things that made friends back in grade school. In college there are no class cut-ups by junior year; they've all flunked out.

4. Stay Awake, Stay Alert

Get enough sleep at night so that you're not sleepy in class. And take your coat and sweater off so you're not cozily warm. Warm rooms, comfortable seats, uniform lighting, and droning professors can't help but induce sleep. You invite trouble if you arrive sleepy and sit in a cocoon of clothing.

Also, no matter how far the instructor digresses, sit up with pen poised, listening for the next word that belongs in your notes. Active listening is the best attention-riveter of all.

CATCH THE LECTURER'S CLUES

As the lecturer speaks, your notes have to convert her words into the following:

- *Main idea:* this word or phrase should head each day's notes. If the lecturer finishes one topic and goes on to another the same day, begin a *new* page with this new main idea. If the lecturer covers one main idea in several lectures, start a new page for each lecture.
- *Subordinate topics:* the pieces that fit together to form the body of the main idea.
- *Supports:* the definitions, explanations, examples, and proofs of all the topic's pieces.

These terms should all be familiar by now; if not, reread Chapter 3.

If the lecturer follows a strict outline, and you've mastered Outline Form, your note-taking job is a snap. The more he tends to ramble and jump around, the tougher it is to take notes. But the following suggestions should help you.

1. Relate the Lecture to Your Assigned Reading

Does the instructor stick closely to the textbook, following it along chapter by chapter and page by page? If so, you can outline or map what'll be covered *before* you go to class, leaving lots of space for inserts as you outline. Then just fill in your notes while you listen.

Does he just zero in on the tricky ideas in your textbook, assuming you can figure out the rest? If so, it's vital to read and take notes on the chapter beforehand.

Does he focus on just the important facts and ideas, adding details and perspectives that aren't in your book? If so, skim the chapter before class and read it carefully afterward, so that when you take chapter notes you'll be able to follow the instructor's thinking and make sense of it.

Do his lectures completely supplement the assigned reading, providing unrelated information you won't find there? Then you've got to take full, careful notes in the lecture hall, but you can read the textbook at your leisure.

2. Keep Track of Time

Time is often a clue to what's important in a lecture. The more time devoted to an idea, the more important the lecturer usually considers it. Are there lots of examples? Is time spent writing on the board? Was time taken to prepare slides and show them on an overhead projector? Is time used to repeat one thought several times in several different ways? Become sensitive to the time factor.

3. Listen for Speaking Style

Most people have a distinctive way of conveying their

thoughts. Once you've decoded a lecturer's style, you can count on the fact that it'll vary only a little during the course. A lecturer who jumps around from thought to thought one day will jump around every day of the year. A lecturer who begins the semester strictly organized can be counted on for fairly strict organization ever after. So take a few minutes after the first lecture to consciously pinpoint your instructor's style.

Some instructors begin every lecture with jokes and digressions as if they had all the time in the world; then, forty minutes into the hour, they realize they haven't covered half of what they need to. Into the last five or ten minutes, quickly and in outline form, they may try to jam up to a half hour's content. Don't be fooled; you'll be expected to know it *all* on the next exam. So get that packed last few minutes' worth into your notes—even if you have to stay after class to fit it all in. It won't be easy, because less savvy students are packing their gear and putting on their coats. But it's worth every mad dash for your next class.

Some instructors, on the other hand, start firing important information as soon as the bell rings, hardly giving you time to unpack your gear. For those courses, it's important to arrive a few minutes early.

Teachers rarely jump into a subject without first either *reviewing* enough to put today's topic into perspective, or *previewing* the subject for today. Some lecturers do both. During a review, check your past notes to see that they're correct. Use a preview to zero in on the main topic that'll head today's notes, and also to jot down a tentative outline. (Leave lots of white space for filling in details.)

Teachers who talk in monotone are a particular hazard. Don't be lulled; instead, consider yourself challenged to take good notes despite the handicap. Like mumblers and racers, they separate the weak note-takers from the strong.

Instructors who speak in unfamiliar accents are the worst problem of all—unless you listen particularly attentively the first few days. Usually what throws us is their different way of speaking particular consonants or vowels. If a professor says, as one of ours did, "the georagy of the Apparachians," you can train your ear to replace every "r" with an "l." If an instructor uses the word "petrol" for oil and "whilst" for while, learn to keep it from distracting your ear from the point he's making.

If you know you have trouble listening attentively, you can train your ear using your phonograph or tape deck. Force yourself to memorize the words of pop songs with as few listenings as possible. If you can decipher the words being sung by a mumbler or screamer, you're set for any class lecturer.

4. Keep Alert for the Lecturer's Special Words

When you take notes on assigned reading, you can put ideas into your own words. But when you take lecture notes, that's not always possible. It's a good idea to copy rules, principles, and other major ideas precisely the way they're said. Also be sure to copy precisely all the course jargon and the lecturer's pet words and phrases. She'll use—and expect you to use—those words on your exams. By the third or fourth lecture, you'll probably have a good idea of what those words are.

In addition, listen for direction words—the words that tell what kind of information is coming. It will help you organize your notes. For instance, "for instance" usually means "here's an example that illustrates the point I just made." This should tell you not just to take down the example, but to make sure that you've recorded the point of it all. Some other direction words are: "to sum up," "therefore," and "in essence," (all meaning "here comes a review of the topic I've been discussing"); "it means" (meaning "this is the definition I expect you to remember"); and "to review" (meaning "this is something I've said before that's important to remember" and implying "it may be on the next exam"). There's no guarantee that direction words *always* work. An instructor may follow "for instance" with a long, rambling digression that doesn't belong in your notes. But learning to listen for these words cuts half the struggle out of lecture note-taking.

7

Taking Research Notes

Most students attempt to use the same system for research notes that they use for their lectures and assigned reading. But it can't be done. Ideally, all the students in a course take down approximately the same lecture and textbook notes. But research is an individual task. Even when several students choose the same topic, they almost never take the same approach or use the same sources. (When they do, the typical professor is likely to look closely for clues to who was copying from whom.)

Research is usually assigned to fill in textbook gaps or to provide greater insight into coursework. In most cases, you're expected to write a paper on the research topic. For assigned reading or lecture notes, you can preview what's coming by glancing at your course outline. For research notes, the only thing you have to start with is a topic.

Our companion book *Research Shortcuts* goes into great detail on how to focus your topic to get the best research results, and on how to find the research materials you need.

Let's assume that you've defined your topic well and that you know how to use research resources. The next thing you must do—before you start researching—is to create a preliminary outline.

PREPARING A PRELIMINARY OUTLINE

The preliminary outline for your paper (or oral report, if that's what you're aiming for) is the first important step in pinpointing the kind of data you need to look for. Prepare the outline in any form you like, but be sure you begin with your main topic. (Here, we like to call the main topic our *working title*. It helps us focus more specifically on the goal of our research.) If we're writing a short, uncomplicated paper, we often just list the subtopics underneath the title without worrying about finding the best order. If it's a long paper, or a complicated one, however, we like to use the outline form shown in Chapter 3.

Don't expect to be able to fill in a complete outline at this point. If you could, you'd have nothing to research. Your outline should contain lots of holes and question marks. But if you don't know enough about your topic to make some sort of outline, do some preliminary reading in an overview volume like an encyclopedia. Researching when you know *nothing* is like trying to mix concrete from scratch when you don't even know what concrete is made of.

To show what we mean, here's an actual preliminary outline we prepared for a 4,000-word article that was later published in *OMNI* magazine.

Working Title: Agent X: Biology's "Subatomic Particle"

1. What is it?
   a. Chemical composition
   b. Where it's found
   c. What diseases it causes (for sure)

2. Evidence it exists
   a. Historical
      ?
      ?
      ?
   b. Now
      1. People working on it
      2. Typical experiments
         ?
         ?
      3. Research techniques being tried
3. Importance of understanding Agent X
   a. To science and medicine
   b. To mankind
   c. To people researching it
      1. Nobel Prizes, etc.

LISTING RESEARCH QUESTIONS

Using your preliminary outline, the next step is to prepare a list of questions to be used as a basic research guide. These questions will be your most important tool. They'll keep you from amassing pages of irrelevant material, and they'll ensure that you continue your research until you have all the information you need. If there are any subtopics in your outline that don't need to be researched, keep them off your question list: for example, topics for which you already have the answers, or which need only your own personal experience or opinion.

As you research, check off each question once you feel you've fully answered it. If one source has the answers to several scattered questions, be sure to check all the questions you've answered or you'll find yourself doubletracking through the same material.

When you're taking notes from someone else's prepared text or lecture, we explained in Chapter 2, you must be able to recognize the *category* into which the information falls: fact or opinion, and if fact what kind of fact. When you're taking notes in order to prepare your own paper or talk, category is *just as important*. For each question on your research list, you must decide what category of answer you need, opinion or fact, and if fact whether you need supporting evidence. In addition, you must decide how up-to-date your answers need to be. Once you know, jot down those guidelines next to each question on your list, and use them to help you plan where and how to do your research.

Exercise

For practice, using our "Agent X" outline, prepare the list of questions you'd need in order to research the article. Compare it with the list we used, which is shown in Appendix G.

USING GOOD NOTE-TAKING TOOLS

Most students' research efforts result in a stack of cards, a heap of assorted papers, a sheaf of photocopies and print-outs, and a pile of books with tagged pages. They lug it all home, and then they first begin to organize. No wonder it all seems so overwhelming. No wonder so many undergrad papers get turned in after deadline.

If you prepare the right materials, you can do all your organizing while you research, right from your list of research questions. It means taking a few minutes extra with each piece of information you find, but it saves hours—even days—in the long run.

If you've found a system that gets you As, stick with it. If you haven't, try ours.

1. Prepare a Work File

Before you compile your first piece of data, prepare a file folder and a looseleaf or spiral-bound notebook, and always keep one inside the other. Paste or staple both your preliminary outline and your list of questions right inside the notebook or folder so that they're protected from loss and wear. Divide your notebook into sections, one section for each question on your list. Tag the sections with the appropriate numbers (from your question list) so you can flip quickly from one section to the other as you find the data that answer each respective question.

Always keep a left-hand margin of an inch or more on every page of notes. That space is for the words and phrases that'll help you, later, to organize your paper. And always write on just one side of the page, so that you'll be able to cut apart your notes and paste them back together in different sequence later when you're writing your paper.

Label your file folder with a one-word or two-word project name, and put your name, address, and phone number on it and on your notebook as a safeguard. Into the folder will go all your photocopies and bibliography sheets (a key tool we'll tell you about next).

Several books on research techniques endorse index cards for note-taking. You can even buy prepackaged cards that have printed title-and-author fill-ins at the top. We recommend them only for super-organized people, the kind who never throw a jacket over a chair and have a special drawer or cubbyhole for everything they own. If you go the card route instead of buying a notebook, purchase the biggest cards you can find so that you're not constantly shuffling them to find the card on which one particular note begins or ends. Then key each card with the number of the question it answers (taken from your question sheet). Keep your cards rubberbanded together and invest in a file envelope instead of a file folder to keep the cards from getting lost.

2. Prepare Bibliography Blanks

Most college paper assignments call for footnotes or a

bibliography. Even for those papers that don't, you'll raise your grades by citing your sources fully in the paper's text. For accurate citation—and, just as important, for a real timesaver—prepare a quantity of bibliography blanks and fill them out as you research, right when you have the sources in front of you. These fill-ins will also help you locate a source quickly if you need to find it again once the books are all back in the stacks.

Using the accompanying illustration on page 71 as a model, type a bibliography master blank on a full-size (8½″ × 11″) sheet of unlined paper. Then photocopy a bunch of blanks and keep them in your file folder. (To save time and money, set up a template in your word processor and print the forms in batches for every research project throughout school.)

For *each* source in your research, fill in a bibliography blank accurately and legibly. You can insert the project title (or an abbreviation) before you begin your research. Give each blank you use a consecutive reference number (the first #1, the second #2, and so on), and keep all the filled-in blanks together in your folder. For books, most of the information can be taken right from the card catalog listing. For periodicals and journals, most of the reference guides give all the information you need. If you use the library stacks for research, the bibliography blanks can double as stack-search tools, taking the place of the scraps of paper you've used in the past to jot down call numbers.

Keep a bibliography sheet for each reference you look at even if you use no information from it. For each rejected reference, under *comment* fill in why you didn't use it. This'll save time and effort if you decide later on that you really needed that reference after all, or if you don't remember whether or not you've looked up a particular book or pamphlet.

Fill in a bibliography blank even if you expect to have the source (book, pamphlet, or whatever) in your possession while you're writing the paper. (For most projects you won't need a book's price so we've put that far down in a corner.)

We've already mentioned several functions served by the bibliography blanks. Let's review the two most important ones.

- For footnotes, you've got all the data together in one set of papers. If you need to make a bibliography, you can alphabetize just by shifting papers around.
- Filling in blanks encourages you to take down all the information you might need immediately when it's available, and to take it down legibly. It saves the hours you formerly spent hunting down one correct spelling or page number.

3. Key Your Notes to the Bibliography Blanks

Once you've filled in a bibliography blank, you're ready to take notes from that source. Turn to your notebook, to the section whose question this note answers and, *before* you begin your notes, *copy down the reference number you've assigned to this source.* Since each bibliography sheet you prepare is given a *reference number,* and no two sheets have the same number, if you remember to begin each note from that reference with its bibliography number *you need never repeat the author or title of the reference again until you get to your paper's final draft.* Think what an enormous time-saver that is.

If you've already learned to keep separate bibliography lists and to just write the author's last name in your notes, continue doing it your way—but add the bibliography reference number as a safeguard. We use both author's last name and bibliography reference number, to make sure we haven't given two references the same number, and to separate the notes from two books by the same author or two authors with the same last name.

Bibliography Master Sheet

Call # _____

Project _____   Reference # _____

Author _____

Editor _____last_____   ____first____   ____init.____

Title of whole _____

Title of part used _____

(Series title) _____

Second authors
    editors _____
_____
_____

Book: Publisher _____

  Where published _____

  Date _____ (Edition #) _____

Periodical: Volume _____ # _____ Date _____

Web site address _____

Web site sponsor _____ Date accessed _____

Forum name (if an online comment) _____

Total pages of whole work _____

Total pages of part used _____

Comments

Used _____

Not Used _____

4. Note Which Page Numbers Your Notes Came From

Have you copied down the bibliography reference
number and the author's last name? Even if you have,

you're still not ready to write that note! First you *must* write down the page number (or numbers) on which the information appears in the source. You'll need those page numbers for footnotes, for supporting your facts if you're challenged, and for finding the same information fast if you ever need it again.

Here's how a typical note of ours looks:

> *#5, Jones, pg. 7.* "It's easy to measure your own heartbeat rate." Put rt. thumb (if l-handed) on l-h wristbone. Keep l-h palm up. *pg. 8.* Now curl r-h index finger around wrist opp. to where thmb is already in postn. Adjst the 2 fngrs untl u feel plse, "generally just above the wristbone."

Notice that *each new page* in our reference is shown in our note. That way, no matter how much or how little we decide to use in the final paper, the footnote will be accurate.

5. Key Each Photocopy and Printout

Most students make too many photocopies. It seems like a time-saver, at the time, to put a nickel or dime in a machine rather than sit for a half hour taking notes. Most of the time, however, if you stop to think about it, you'll find that all that's really relevant and important on the page is a line or two. Once you get your giant sheaf of photocopies home, you're only going to have to do the reading and culling you could have done instead of standing in line to use the machine.

Some references that you need will be so long, it does make sense to photocopy or print them: for instance, if you think you'll be using several paragraphs from a source word-for-word. Fill in the bibliography sheets for each source you photocopy and then, *while* you're at the machine, immediately write on each photocopy itself (1) the bibliography reference number, (2) the page number of the source of this photocopy, and (3) if you like safeguards, the author's last name.

Be sure to keep all photocopies and printouts in the file folder along with your notebook, so they don't get lost or mislaid.

KEEPING NOTES LEGIBLE

Most people begin a project taking notes carefully and legibly. But soon the pen gets hard to hold and handwriting becomes tight and cramped. The letters become smaller, closer together, harder to read. Nobody's immune from note-taker's scribble.

If you're bent in the direction of frugality, now is not the time to let it lead you. Never attempt to cram more notes on the page than its lines can hold. Stay on the lines as if they were walls. They'll help keep your letters large enough to be legible. And skip a line between notes so that later you can pinpoint each source quickly. (It'll also make cutting and pasting easier, if that's part of your paper-preparing style.)

If your words still tend to squeeze as the day lengthens, make yourself write on every *other* line. It really does keep your letters larger. In that case, skip *two* lines between references to separate them at a glance.

If, despite all precaution, you still end up with illegible notes, use a looseleaf notebook instead of a spiral one, and try typing all your notes. Some libraries have soundproof research rooms to which you can bring your own computer, and some even have rental computers for hire at reasonable rates.

Do use the note-taking shorthand you've developed, but *don't* start using new symbols and abbreviations the first time for a research project—unless you're willing to keep a glossary of these shortcuts in your notebook as you go along. Otherwise, your notes may be unintelligible by the time you need them.

TAKING ADEQUATE NOTES

No amount of preparation can guarantee that when you've done all your research and begin to write that paper, you'll have absolutely everything you need in hand. Most of the time, there's at least one small example or quotation that needs to be tracked down to support some new idea that has crept into the first draft. But if you've taken time with the preliminary outline and the list of research questions, those holes should be minimal—so long as you take adequate notes.

If what you're copying is statistical, or composed of other hard facts, it's tempting to just jot down the information the moment you find it, and to go right on to the next question on your list. However, first make sure you've got *all* the information, not just the bare facts but also the provisos and limiters that make it true (or true only some of the time). You can be sure of that only if you take the time to skim paragraphs which surround that piece of information.

Since we rarely know when we'll need a direct quote and when just a paraphrase will do, we take many of our notes *in the source's own words*. Then, to remind us that we've copied exactly, we put quotation marks around these words. It's a practice we highly recommend.

We often find, by the time we get to the last few questions on the research list, that they've already been answered in the course of other research. But before we pack our gear and head home, we double-check that list. The checks and double-checks are what make this system foolproof.

8

Taking Minutes of Meetings

The one kind of note-taking most likely to be used once a student leaves school—and least likely to be taught anywhere along the line—is the taking of minutes at meetings. And it's a very valuable skill, too. The person who can confidently offer to take the minutes of the volunteer group's meeting is sure to be nominated for president of the organization in the not-too-distant future. The worker who knows how to take good minutes of a meeting does not long go unnoticed by the boss.

Taking good minutes is akin to taking good lecture notes—but there's more to it. For one thing, everything that's officially part of the meeting belongs in the minutes, no matter how irrelevant or unimportant it may seem to you. And in addition to being responsible for recording what's being said, quickly, accurately, and briefly, you must take down other vital information as well. While many organizations rely on tape recorders to get the words correct, there's no substitute for a good minutes-taker to supply the rest of the information. We'll list what to look and listen for. Make sure to get it all in your minutes.

1. Time, place, and purpose of the meeting.
2. Name and title of meeting chairperson.
3. Number of members at the meeting. (This number is particularly important if the organization's bylaws call for a *quorum* to conduct business or pass motions.)
4. If names are important, names of members attending the meeting, as well as their titles or organizational affiliations (if that's important). The easiest way to collect this information is for the minutes-taker to pass around a sign-in sheet and let each member present fill in her own name and title or affiliation.

Points 1 through 4 are usually written in at the head of the meeting's minutes. The points that follow (5 through 9) tell exactly what happened at the meeting, in the order in which it happened. Although you can jot down the notes in half-sentences and shorthand, the final version may have to be written more formally, in sentence format. Often, however, an expanded outline format is perfectly all right. Find out how minutes of a particular group were prepared in the past and stick to that style.

5. Names (and titles) of all people who present reports, along with summaries of their reports.
6. All motions, in exactly the wording they are presented, and all amendments in their exact wording. The minutes must name the maker of each motion and each amendment, as well as the names of the people who second these motions and amendments.
7. The names of all the people who are recognized by the chair to speak on motions, amendments, or other business, along with summaries of their remarks. If

anyone speaks without being recognized by the chair, those remarks do *not* belong in the minutes.

8. The names of all guest speakers, with summaries of their statements.
9. A record of all votes taken, along with the number of people voting *yes, no,* and *abstaining.*

The following two pieces of information belong at the end of a meeting's minutes.

10. The time of adjournment.
11. The name, title (if any), and signature of the person who took the minutes. If a different person typed the minutes, that name should appear as well.

The best organization aid a minutes-taker can find is the *agenda,* the outline for the meeting that the chair usually prepares in advance. If there's an agenda, be sure you get a copy of it at the start of the meeting. But be flexible: the agenda is only a guideline, not a guarantee. Time, space, or whim may cause the meeting to veer greatly from it.

Despite all precautions, inaccuracies sometimes do creep into minutes. That's why there will usually be an opportunity near the start of the next business meeting to have minutes read and either corrected or approved as read. Don't be thrown if your minutes have to be corrected. Even the Congress makes corrections to minutes taken by professional minutes-takers. Like all note-taking, the taking of minutes is a skill that practice perfects.

Appendix A: Notes on Chapter 1

WHY TAKE GOOD NOTES

1. helps you pay attention
   a. prepackaged notes = problems
      1. mind wanders
      2. may be incomplete
   b. tape recorder problems
      1. mind wanders
      2. garbling & mechanical problems
      3. need transcribe or rehear
2. helps remember
   a. it's muscle activity
         ex. = bike-riding
3. helps organize ideas
   a. diff. between overzealous, undeveloped, & just right

Appendix B: Practice in Analyzing Information and Taking Notes on Lectures

In the following speech, opinion words are <u>underlined</u>, irrelevancies are ~~crossed out~~, evidence is placed in (parenthesis), and categories of evidence—as well as other explanatory remarks—are shown in the left-hand margin. When we asked Dr. Plesur for permission to use his speech—which he has given in several revised forms since this first rendering a decade ago—he noted several revisions that he'd make if this were to be published as part of an actual paper. The speaker, you'll notice, was able to offer evidence with scanty citation of sources because of his reputation as a historian. Unless you're an acclaimed expert, you'd better make your citations complete. (At the end of the speech, you'll find additional notes to accompany the exercise on outlining.)

~~We historians are not in vogue nowadays, so when I have an audience even semi-captured like this it's an inviting, enticing kind of situation to be in. But this is~~

81

going to be a history lecture and I hope some of you will be transported nostalgically to your past history.

Evidence is corroborative: we can assume many people heard her.

In an obvious state of rancor, Gloria Steinem, appearing recently before the National Press Club, called President Nixon the most sexually insecure chief of state since Napoleon. Ms. Steinem's remark was her reaction to the President's less than enthusiastic stand, (we are told) on women's liberation.

Evidence is incomplete: "we are told" BY WHOM is left out.

This contretemps points up a subject, I think, little studied by the social historian who after all is concerned primarily with mores, morals, and in general what (we call) popular culture.

Evidence only authoritative if WE are considered authorities.

Despite the disdain Americans claim they have for history and the assertions of popular intellectuals and others that the discipline is irrelevant to today's action, I think most Americans are down deep and maybe even in a sublimated way lovers of the past. Legends or facts about our chief executives, true stories or fascinating gossip, and unfortunately even salacious banter, excite both the curious and the scholarly.

This sentence is authoritative evidence for the prior sentence. Notice that a complete citation is made.

(Gore Vidal has stated in a recent review, I believe it was of the excellent book about Franklin and Eleanor Roosevelt by Joseph Lash, he stated in a recent *New York Review of Books* article that there exists a large public curiosity as to the happenings in the White House bedrooms or even in the corridors outside.) The world is fascinated by the exploits of the famous and since sexuality obviously colors our lives, since it affords a unique insight into a person, president or not, I think it's the duty of the student to also explore this aspect of presidential lifestyle.

One of the trends of my discipline, not that I really understand it that much, is the study of psychohistory. And ever since Sigmund Freud, of course, sex has been the major part of the psychic profile that now, years later, historians are developing concerns with.

If a politician behaves in a certain way in his private life, there's a possibility that he could act in a similar

Evidence for prior sentence, both pro & con. Notice that the evidence is, however, qualified as OPINION & is therefore not strong evidence. Also it is incomplete because no citations are given.

Source of evidence not cited.

vein publicly. And, ~~of course,~~ private indiscretions can eventually affect public policy. (The famous example of Charles Stuart Parnell in Ireland being named a co-respondent in a divorce suit probably hurt his whole program of home loan, but thus far his latterday colleague Bernadette Devlin doesn't seem to have her public life blighted by her private life.) If we're looking for examples, there are many in history.

Today's society (has been called) the most permissive one in modern history, and while there is still a greater expectation of higher morality, I think, in the national leader, and the tendency to equate public greatness with private goodness, there is also more tolerance of a politician's personal weakness. Certainly people tend to overlook what they want to overlook. Some politicians, in other words, have fared better than others. Perhaps the presidential libido can even be rationalized, since men at the top (are reputed) to have very strong drives of many kinds or else they would not have achieved that eminence. And then there's also the unprecedented strain on the man in public life, in essence, which could explain, perhaps, the need for private release. ~~I didn't explore that in a previous article on presidential health, and if I put these two papers together, the one on physical health and this on sexual health, I may go into this more.~~

But despite all that I have said was so important about sexuality in further understanding the President, the richness of psychoanalytic speculation is not matched by the historical evidence. We live in an age of media, and the less responsible of members of the press have always scrutinized, sometimes in very indelicate ways, every aspect of the presidential image.

You know, the president is no more than an elected king as far as many Americans are concerned and we are obviously fascinated by every little detail and every little fact, and perhaps the more salacious ones are more important to the layman than perhaps items of policy. The man in public life has not been entitled to an exclusive private life, and whispering galleries work overtime in producing rumors of politicians' possible real and imagined sexual derelictions. The American president is usually pretty well insulated against excessively prying eyes. There were at least two presidents for whom we now have fairly good documentation about their extramarital sexual affairs. (Warren G. Harding used the Secret Service evidently to watch over his White House frolics, and while the second Roosevelt's marriage was almost broken up over his dalliance, it was kept out of print.) The stories about John Kennedy's fascination with pretty girls were common Washington stories, but no scandal ever ensued. ~~And I would predict, even though~~ historians ought not to, that it would ~~probably~~ take a long time for any scandal to break.

Cleveland's victory was due in part to the blemished reputation of his adversary and to his own spotless record. As President, at the age of 49, his marriage to a 22-year-old girl in the year 1886 aroused great comment. In fact, I think, a lot of the society columnists were a little aggravated and tiffed because they thought that he was going to marry the girl's mother. Instead he married her. Mean gossips were full of gossip about beauty and the beast, but the marriage was a fine one and there was nothing to indicate anything but an exemplary moral life. Indeed, he sired his last child at the age of 70. He died the next year.

Woodrow Wilson complained of his ignorance of women and yet he (was reputed to be) a man of strong passion. His only real sexual interest was the woman he married in 1885. There were persisting stories about Mr. Wilson, especially in the few months after his wife died, but no story was more exciting than his romance with a 43-year-old beautiful widow, Edith Bolling

Marginal notes:

Evidence incomplete—no documentation.

This is NOT evidence for previous statement.

Evidence for "aroused great comment"—but not very complete.

Evidence incomplete.

Evidence incomplete. Gault. Wilson proposed marriage to her. During this ardent courtship, he (was criticized) for emphasizing affairs of the heart and neglecting those of state. (Some **Authoritative evidence for prior statement.** of his daily letters to Mrs. Gault were 20 pages in length.) Now that took time, I suppose, away from the presidential burden.

Now this next section is going to deal with those presidents about whom there are interesting stories, about whom there may be implications and suspicions—although I add that the supportive evidence is weak and much of what I'm going to say is pre-presidential in chronology.

Authoritative but incomplete. George Washington first, ~~naturally.~~ He was described (by most of his biographers) as an awkward and an unsuccessful young lover, a condition that for the most **Authoritative but incomplete.** part, (as I read about Washington), did not improve with his age. (A critical biographer, writing ~~incidentally~~ in the debunking era of the 1920s, actually theorized that **Evidence: authority. (But notice that he questions authority.)** Washington's idealization of women was in fact a disappointment to most women because, according to this amateur and maybe frustrated psychologist, women do not like this kind of behavior.) (Washington's many **Evidence: authority. (But does it prove the next part of the sentence?)** letters are replete with references to frustrating experiences) and therefore he felt wise enough to give advice on love and sex and marriage, ~~and if time permitted I could read to you from some of those letters.~~ Possibly his major sexual interest was the wife of a dear friend, **This parenthetical statement IS germane to the lecture's topic.** Mrs. Sally Fairfax. Forty years after their initial meeting (George didn't give up too easily), he wrote her in Paris.

I think it is interesting to point out that Washington, Jefferson, and Madison all married widows. ~~Maybe I'll have more to say about that later.~~

Authoritative, but evidence incomplete. (A lengthy article) talks about Washington's subliminal relationships with his own brother, an older brother that died when Washington was just 20, with a frontiersman with whom he served, and even with Alexander Hamilton, but I don't think we should push these points by any means. These were certainly hardly consummated relationships.

John Adams, with typical honesty, admitted that he thoroughly enjoyed the fair sex. Although Adams appears to have been quite a ladies' man—(he used to recite ovids to the art of love to various people)—(he claimed, "No virgin or matron ever had cause to blush at the sight of me or to regret her acquaintance with me. No father, brother, son, or friend ever had cause for grief or resentment for any intercourse between me and any daughter, sister, mother, or any other relation of the female sex.")Now there isn't any other president who has written anything that definitive, though I'm sure there are many that could have.

Thomas Jefferson—his love affairs have been (well documented.) Though they were generally unsuccessful, there was at least one that seemed serious—(this is the famous Walker affair)—so much so that (a generation afterwards he acknowledged his guilt and the incorrectness of offering "love to a handsome lady.") In 1772 he married a widow. While it was a happy marriage, Mrs. Jefferson was sick for the ten years that they were married. There were, however, persistent rumors and reports of his use of female slaves. (One such instance that gained tremendous notoriety was the affair with a slave girl named Sally Hennings. His political opposition, of course, made much of this affair. (Now Sally Hennings bore him, so we think, between three and five children. In Jefferson's will there is the well-known provision that there will be five slaves emancipated—I assume Sally and four of her offspring.)

Abraham Lincoln is one of the most thoroughly researched presidents. (According to William Herndon, his ex-law partner, and not the best source, Lincoln had a terribly strong passion for women and even a powerful lust.(The oft-told story of his visit to a lady of

Margin notes:

Evidence incomplete.

Evidence: authority. (But again, citation incomplete.)

Evidence incomplete.

Evidence incomplete.

Authoritative but incomplete.

Evidence without citation.

This continues as part of above evidence (the will). But evidence is diluted by phrase of opinion.

Evidence: authority.

Evidence: authority. See citation in next paragraph.

the night reflects also his basic sense of values and honesty. ~~I hope none of this alarms any of you people who think that I'm doing disservice to President Lincoln.~~ It seems as if he didn't have enough money for the transaction, and when she offered to trust him for the difference, he said that he could not go on credit and he left with his mission incomplete.) ~~I don't know if this is the beginning of the phrase "Honest Abe"—or not, but it certainly could have been.~~

(Now, this is a story that has been told <u>with some degree of plausibility</u> in a <u>respectable</u> historian's work on Lincoln called *The Lincoln Nobody Knows,* by Professor Richard Kirk.)

Now the last president that I want to say something about is the murdered John Kennedy, ~~this despite the~~

Evidence not cited. ~~fact that in Camelot, as you know, the weather must be perfect all the year. Now (we know) that it is not completely perfect (because anybody with the name of Kennedy is fair copy. Senator Ted Kennedy's Chappaquiddick adventure jolted many Americans) but one article stated that half of the women didn't believe what had happened at Chappaquiddick and the other half were dying to forgive him. Jackie's halo has become somewhat tarnished since the marriage to Onassis, the photos of her sporting a no-bra look, and her jet-set~~

Evidence for next part of sentence. Lecturer assumes listeners find this to be self-evident. ~~lifestyle.~~ (Because the President's life ended tragically, and since he has grown larger in death) Americans prefer to disregard the threatening clouds hovering over his area of Camelot. ~~His younger days were spent in the shadow of an older brother, Joe.~~ He ~~and fellow Senator George Smathers of Florida~~ were <u>reputed</u> to

Evidence incomplete. have far outdistanced all competitors in romantic

Evidence authoritative. conquests. <u>Certainly</u> (the society columns) linked this most <u>eligible</u> bachelor with <u>very attractive</u> society

Evidence from a more authoritative source than above. belles. And then there's the <u>revelation</u> of (his long-time secretary Evelyn Lincoln, who said) that one of her duties was to arrange for dates.

Fact by popular definition.

The bachelor's life, of course, ended (with that <u>dream</u> marriage to Jacqueline Bouvier), but it is <u>doubtful</u> that the good life ended for either of them. (The frequent

Self-evident? Lecturer assumes the listener's knowledge.

absences of each from the other) <u>seemed</u> to fuel <u>notions</u> of (those that saw) in the marriage a less than perfect liaison. (A contemporary journalist only recently revived

Evidence incomplete (WHO saw something?).

the <u>old story</u> about John Kennedy's <u>supposed</u> relation-ship with Marilyn Monroe. The movie star <u>was even</u>

Evidence: authority (but journalist not named).

<u>supposed to have</u> credited her peculiar talents for making his back feel better—that's a direct quote. ~~I'd sure like to be the historian that finds the sources on this one.~~

Above information now cited as evidence for this paragraph. Is it fully adequate?

But the <u>implications</u> of (the Kennedy story) illustrate one of the major themes of this paper: discounting sources of the sensational stripe, or hearsay evidence, it is difficult to find positive information about the social adventures of the Chief Executive.

In final statement, in conclusion, the question of what effect a presidential sexual life has upon national politics is hard to answer. <u>I don't think</u> it will ever be definitively answered. All I do tonight is to raise the question. <u>Certainly</u> (Sigmund Freud and his disciples)

Evidence: authority but incomplete (which disciples?).

spoke of the sexual and the power drives, ~~and this whole subject is something I want to think through a little more but it's exciting and even titillating to at least mention it.~~

<u>I think</u> two points need to be made. ~~One I've~~

Evidence: authority.

~~repeated so often (as to be like the woman in Shake-speare) who protested too much. I cannot reiterate it too often, however,~~ and that is that historians must be very, very careful when treading over territory that is known to be full of quicksand, and this is one of those subjects. The hard sources are not readily available. And yet, this fact notwithstanding, the subject deserves attention and study. Sexuality, like medical and health problems in general, is a complex and a dynamic influence which is <u>very obvious</u>, in fact <u>so obvious</u> as to be little realized and <u>certainly</u> seldom spoken of, and even more rarely committed to writing. And yet this factor <u>undoubtedly</u> helps shape personality and while impossible to measure with precision, <u>must have had</u> some effect on the course of presidential administrations.

CLUE WORDS AND NOTES ON SPEECH EXCERPT "EROS IN THE WHITE HOUSE"

Main Topic: sexual lives of the presidents

why study psychohistory?
1. People are curious about subject
   a. Gore Vidal review of Joseph Lash bk on F. & E. Roosevelt in NY Rev of Bks
2. Gives insight into presidents
3. Historians practicing Psychohistory

when begun
   a. developed since Freud
   b. because private lives affect publ policy
      1. Parnell—divorce co-respondent, home-loan program hurt(?)
      2. Devlin—no effect
   c. because pvt behavr might become publ behavr

citizens' attitudes
4. Attitude of citizens
   a. expect morality (tho less today)
   b. equate publ greatness & pvt goodness
   c. harsher toward some presidents
   d. rationalize (?)
      1. one of many strong drives
      2. need to relieve strain of office
   e. Media: always been some scrutiny

definite examples: extramarital affairs, marriage scandals
5. Extramarital affairs
   a. Harding (Secret Service)
   b. F. Roosevelt
   c. JFK (no proof)
6. Scandalous marriage

    a. Cleveland: 49, to 22: 1886 (beauty & beast); child at 70

    b. Wilson: Edith Bolling Gault, 43, daily letters to 20 pgs ("emphasizing affairs of heart & neglecting those of state")

where weak evidence 7. Where evidence weak

    a. Washington: "awkward & unsuccessful lover," idealized women; W. letters tell of "frustrating experiences," i.e. advice-giver

       1. Sally Fairfax, friend's wife, wrote 40 yrs later in Paris

       2. older bro, frontiersman & Hamilton: speculation

    b. Adams: ladies' man: ovids. But wrote that never caused virgin or matron to "blush at sight of me or regret acqu w me" etc.

    c. Jefferson:

       1. Walker affair

       2. m'd widow 1772, she sick 10 yrs after

       3. Sally Hennings, slave, 3–5 chldrn, in will

    d. Lincoln:

       1. passion, lust: ex-law ptnr Wm Herndon

       2. whore & not enough money—told in "Lncln Nobody Knows" by Prof Richard Kirk

    e. Kennedy:

       1. when senator: linked w "society belles," secy Evelyn Lincoln arranged dates

       2. marriage to J Bouvier (not good?)

         a. M Monroe—back rub(?)

8. Effect of sex life on natl politics? conclusion conclusion, may have some effect

    a. hard evidence hard to find

    b. but shld be studied

Appendix C: Course Outline for "Methods of Note-Taking"

1. Why take gd notes
2. What to put down
3. Note-taking aids
4. How to organize
   a. Outline form
   b. Patterning
5. Note-taking shortcuts
6. Taking assigned-text notes
   a. fiction
   b. textbooks
   c. other nonfiction
7. Lecture notes
8. Research notes
9. Meeting minutes

Appendices D and E: Speech Outline and Speech Clue Words

We organized the notes in Appendix B into outline form, and in the left-hand margins we placed our Memory Clue words, so turn to Appendix B to check your answers for these two exercises.

Appendix F: Shorthand Notes on Chapter 4

Main Topic: Note-Taking Shortcuts

1. Omit periods
2. Use tech smbls
   × = times, mltpld by
3. Std abbrevs
   cf = compare
4. Own abbrevs (bettr fr lngr wds)
   a. no vwls
      bkgd = background
   b. wd beginngs only
      assoc = associate
5. –s = plur
   +s = plusses, advntgs
6. Bld systm slowly

Appendix G: "Agent X" Research Questions

The following questions were compiled after preliminary research into the topic. Your questions will probably be much less precise than ours.

1. virus? If so, DNA? RNA? authority
2. chemical composition? definition
3. infects? merges with cells? parasite? authority
4. evolution—what keeps reservoir of Agent X alive? try for experimental evidence
5. how it causes diseases? kuru? CJD? scrapie? others? authority
6. discoverer? citation
7. labs: NY, San Francisco, others? authority
8. research techniques in use? authority

9. proof that it exists? mice? cell culture? direct report
10. importance to science? authority
11. importance to mankind? my conclusion
12. Nobel race? other benefits to researchers? quotes from researchers

Data needed: all most up-to-date except #6.